T0196064

The Victory
Dance of God

HIS PROMISE OF HEALING IS YOURS!

Seven Kingdom Principles That Will Transform Your Life

MARY FRANCES MCMAHON

WESTBOW
PRESS®
A DIVISION OF THOMAS NELSON
& ZONDERVAN

WestBow Press books may be ordered through booksellers or by contacting:

WestBow Press
A Division of Thomas Nelson & Zondervan
1663 Liberty Drive
Bloomington, IN 47403
www.westbowpress.com
1 (866) 928-1240

THE HOLY BIBLE, NEW INTERNATIONAL VERSION®, NIV®
Copyright © 1973, 1978, 1984, 2011 by Biblica, Inc.®
Used by permission. All rights reserved worldwide.

ISBN: 978-1-9736-0527-0 (sc)
ISBN: 978-1-9736-0529-4 (hc)
ISBN: 978-1-9736-0528-7 (e)

Library of Congress Control Number: 2017914984

Print information available on the last page.

WestBow Press rev. date: 5/25/2018

Acknowledgements

For my beautiful husband; love of my life, joy, life's partner, and friend.
Thank you for your love and faithfulness over the years.
We've weathered many storms together
yet through the grace and mercy of God
are better for it.
These writings hold a special place in my heart for you.

Special thanks to my dear sister Gemma.
I owe you a depth of gratitude for your love,
dedication, and commitment to
The Victory Dance of God.
Your professional editing suggestions
meant the world to me.

Finally, to all the elders, men and women pastors, and
ministers at Compassion Christian Church in
Savannah, Georgia.
Thank you for pouring Jesus's love into me these past eleven years.
My heart is indebted to each of you.
May the *Victory Dance of God* be the fruit of your labor.

I dedicate this book to God, my Heavenly Father.
You are so amazing.
How could I have ever doubted?

Contents

The Healing Declaration

As you read the *Victory Dance of God* I proclaim God's covenant of healing over you in body, mind, and spirit.

I declare under the authority of Christ, that His faithful promise of healing is yours.

I affirm through God's word that His love, and power is present to rebuild you, transform you, and make you whole.

I release under this authority His rite of healing; its appointed time, season, and manifestation—to which *you* are called.

I decree that the Holy Spirit will reveal supernatural wisdom to you according to God's divine plans, and purposes for your life.

I declare that every spiritual assault on your life or manifestation by the forces of evil will now be severed and cancelled, according to His word, never to return—in the name of Jesus.

I proclaim that every stronghold will cease and desist, every spiritual, mental, or physical condition will be healed according to His divine design for you through the supernatural, miraculous, extraordinary or ordinary.

I take captive and obedient to Christ, every thought, word or action in you, through you, or around you, that does not serve His purposes, and I place them before His throne to be disposed of in accordance with His word, His power, and sovereignty over your life.

I authorize through His power and authority, that every grip, soul tie, or generational stronghold that has been imposed upon you through sin, or the forces and influences of evil be cut off, and made null and void in the name of Jesus.

I affirm that this declaration is complete, confirmed in the realm of the spirit, and approved under the authority of His word, through the covenant of Christ's death and resurrection. May His mighty right arm of protection be upon you now.

In the name of Jesus, I declare this healing and transformation complete in your life.

Receive the infilling of His Holy Spirit! Be Healed!

The Proclamation of Promises

The Father's plan for salvation and healing was established from the beginning of the world, created specifically for you!

God's word brings forgiveness and repentance from sin, and healing from diseases of the body, mind, and spirit.

Jesus's protection manifests itself in your life, and others' lives through seen, and unseen ways.

God has the ultimate blueprint of healing for you, despite the discouragement or setbacks you may face. You need only access them!

The authority and power of Jesus Christ will change your situation, and bring victory in your life even in impossible situations; through the supernatural, miraculous, extraordinary, or the ordinary.

God's wisdom, through His Holy Spirit, can help you identify generational curses, spiritual, mental, or physical strongholds, and remove them through His power, scriptural promises, superior authority, and redemptive blood covenant with Jesus.

You will be empowered by revelations from God through His Holy Spirit as He confirms His word for you through scripture, dreams, and prophecy.

You will never be held back due to misfortune, illness or tragedy of the world, flesh or devil. As a child of God, if you stay the course, He will use all things for His divine purposes to bring your spiritual destiny to completion.

You will experience relief from medical, physical, emotional, mental or spiritual hardships through the power of His grace, which brings wisdom, perseverance, restoration, and protection.

God's spiritual, mental, emotional, relational, and physical healing is yours, despite any worry, illness or brokenness you've experienced!

I claim *The Victory Dance of God* in you, over you, and around you through salvation, and pray that the marvelous works of God will be manifested in your life in powerful, and fruitful ways.

> "This is the confidence we have in approaching God: that if we ask anything according to his will, he hears us. And if we know that he hears us—whatever we ask—we know that we have what we asked of him."
>
> (I John 5: V 14 - 15)

Author's Remarks

As a healthcare professional for over thirty-eight years, I've witnessed God's healing power manifested time and again in the lives of courageous men, women, and children.

I've experienced first-hand, God's tenderness, mercy, and healing in my own life, despite the diagnosis of an incurable form of cancer. I've heard miraculous stories of God's love and faithfulness in the lives of men and women I've served. I've witnessed God's mighty hand perform extraordinarily in the lives of sick family members, friends, and people groups I've helped in the world. In each circumstance, Jesus remained faithful to deliver His promises in conformity with His word, divine plans, and purposes.

In my book, *The Victory Dance of God, His Promise of Healing is Yours,* my prayer is that you will:

1. Gain treasured knowledge about God's nature and personality;
2. Grasp His power and ability to answer your intimate requests for healing;
3. Understand perfect spiritual wisdom through kingdom principles, and apply these tenets to experience powerful restoration in your life; and
4. Engage in spiritual warfare through the authority of His word to break generational strongholds, and halt physical, mental, and spiritual affliction.

When you establish or rekindle a life-changing relationship with Christ, you'll not only open the door to His promises, your life will transform before your eyes.

Your intimate relationship with Him will catapult your health. You'll undergo a body, mind, and heart lift. You'll develop fortitude and resilience. You'll rise above life's toughest challenges. You'll complete your God-given destiny in accordance with His perfect plans for your life. This is *"The Victory Dance of God"* over you! Believe!

Introduction to *The Victory Dance of God*
We Are Never Beyond Repair

During my travels to the jungles of South America some years back, I discovered an abandoned shack situated on the muddy water's edge near the heart of the Amazon river basin.

The aged structure was in shambles. Most of the cracked tree sticks that had bolstered the house above the dirt foundation were eroded, mildewed, or twisted from repeated pounding of severe storms. Further, much of the ruined structure above the groundwork had simply collapsed into decaying piles of rotting wood.

I was tempted to pry the warped door open, and step inside the crumbling room behind the face of the entrance but decided against it. The house was essentially wrecked, yet I imagined life was lived there by some man, woman or child who inhabited the inner room called "home." The debilitated condition of the building left me sad-struck. It was a stark reminder of the perilous storm conditions waged against my own inner house leaving me at times emotionally battered, weary, and in need of spiritual and bodily repairs.

The *Victory Dance of God* has been years in the making. Squalls, winds, and relentless storms cost delays in its wake. Nonetheless, just like the storm-tossed apostles who battled gale force winds with fear and trepidation while in their boat, my spiritual journey through the storms of life delayed the timing of this work.

Truth is, we've all fallen short of the glory of God. If we're human, sin, faults and mistakes will have their way with us. Struggles erupt through the flesh, leaving permanent marks for some, while for others, opportunities for rebuilding, and spiritual growth.

Our human condition is a given, and so is depravity in body, mind, and spirit until we return home to our natural state.

Being fallen means more than consciously, and actively separating ourselves from God. Our faulty nature deposits a cloud of unknowing in us, preventing us from spiritually grasping the full redemptive nature of God while we are in the flesh, or having a perfect relationship with Him originally shared by Adam and Eve before the great fall. Due to man's relationship with God handed-down through the original blood lines from the first family, God's ultimate will for us to be in perfect relationship with Him in the garden, realigned through an alternate plan of saving through the redemptive sacrifice of Jesus. Thus, our spiritual relationship was restored, conferring desperately needed redemption along with spiritual, mental, and physical healing for us, and yes—even access to His divine power.

Even though our lives are lived out in an often messy and chaotic world, Jesus's death and resurrection liberated us from the weight of our earthly curse. You don't have to beg for what He's already purchased for you on the cross. When God brings healing, favor or pours grace into your life, it's done. He's sovereign over all of it; shifting and mixing the negative aftereffects of your life into a divine soup that bolsters the spirit, transforms your mind, changes the heart, heals your body, and rescues you from the insensible, and often painful events which cause confusion, and hopelessness in your world. His favor and blessing impart healing, grace, supernatural, miraculous, extraordinary and grace-filled interventions, financial stability, strength in body, mind, and spirit, freedom through challenges, peace amidst adversity, cooperation, agreement in difficult situations, and perseverance during crisis. Most times this occurs in a way that is exactly opposite to how we think or expect He's going to intervene.

While our fallen nature places a barrier between us, and our spiritual growth, the greater power of God's redemption in us can overcome it. This is the nature of grace. It nudges and reminds us of His unfailing love. It's telling of His power, time and again. Though we lack spiritual fortitude, grace relentlessly knocks on the door of our heart, inviting us enter the chamber of His.

Having a relationship with God is more than a one-night stand. It requires diligence, commitment, and a spiritual pact, permitting Him to reconstruct us from the ground up through a series of rearrangements which shake the old, and create the new. The work is wearing without grace. It requires jack-hammering, tearing down of rooms, rebuilding of inner walls, repairing outside structures, and reconstructing in us a solid foundation, so we can wholly transform into the Godly men and women He desires us to become.

Make no mistake, rebuilding and restructuring from the inside out is a labor of love which involves more than the physical. It requires first and foremost, a stripping-away, laying bare the core of one's heart, exposing the very depth of one's disposition toward the master builder. If we truly want to be whole, it compels us to "become born again," a subject which mystified even Nicodemus.

> "How can a man be born when he is old?" Nicodemus asked. "Surely he cannot enter a second time into his mother's womb to be born!"
>
> (John 3: V 4)

Scripture shares there is a powerful connection between the health of man, healing, and *rebirth* through a relationship with Jesus. Our ability to be completely whole is tightly woven with our redemption: both understanding the secret depths of our heart toward God, and God's perfect heart toward us.

> "As water reflects a face, so a man's heart reflects the man."
>
> (Proverbs 27: V 19)

> "The good man brings good things out of the good stored up in his heart, and the evil man brings evil things out of the evil stored up in his heart. For out of the overflow of his heart his mouth speaks."
>
> (Luke 6: V 45)

> "I will give you a new heart and put a new spirit in you; I will remove from you your heart of stone and give you a heart of flesh. And I will put my spirit in you and move you to follow my decrees and be careful to keep my laws."
>
> (Ezekiel 36: V 26 - 27)

Our rebirth then, launches a *lifetime of healing* for us in relationship with Jesus. It's our make-over, necessary overhaul, refurbishment, and repair of our spiritual inner home. It's the state of grace in which we relearn our knowing of Him, link up with the powers that be (Father, Son, and Holy Spirit), experience His heartfelt love, and recapture intimate connections after seasons of faithlessness, and distancing ourselves from Him. It's newfound time between the lover (Him), and the beloved (you), a dwelling place where fresh beginnings recapture the mind, rejuvenate the heart, and restore the spirit through the eyes of His redeeming love, over and over.

Healing is nearer than you think. You'll recognize it when it happens. It's a place where broken bonds are mended, wounds are repaired and sutured, and a time of seasonal upswing when self-destructive activity goes off the grid. Personal resurrection and overhaul gives way to firsthand stories of living-out in novel and exciting ways, the clean slate, while new plans and purposes are birthed inside you.

Make no mistake, redemption is bona fide, but so is spiritual warfare. There are flames inside us which never die, and inner battles we wage against which are endless due to our human nature. We are deeply marked by our flesh. Rebellion serves to remind us of the original fall, predisposing us to the giving into things we fight so hard to resist.

God made us in His image and likeness, but we still defy. We are redeemed yet fallen, spiritually awakened yet self-deceived, immersed in light but grasping the dark. Holy, nevertheless marked with stain. Our human dependencies are real yet at best unreliable, redundant, and powerless.

The storms and winds in life will have their way with us if we let them. When we spiritually build on the cheap, there will always be breaking and ripping away of things after the fury has passed. Human tempests cause serious damage in their wake. They leave us battered and bewildered in an aftermath of ruin while we scramble to recoup our losses. The scourge of shattered dreams, emotional hits, bad breaks or physical illness do not have to win the day. Although the schemes and tactics of the enemy (satan) are meant to destroy and crush you, God, and the devil assemble tools with different purposes in mind. The two are on unequal footing.

Repair, redemption, and redesign are the devil's enemies. He specializes in demolishing us permanently. Either we grant satan a foothold and allow him to snatch us from the truth of God's love and the power of His death and resurrection, or arm ourselves with seven-kingdom principles to empower us, standing firm on the foundation of Gods redemptive power to heal and restore us.

A downward spiraling effect occurs when we convince ourselves that God is absent, doesn't care, isn't listening or we've been dealt a raw deal. We spend countless hours stewing in anger or self-pity, feeling spent from living lives on our own terms rather than God's power. The gale force winds we encounter are meant to challenge us into wakefulness, and invite us to change our ways. Instead, we allow them to rob us of the magnificent prize Jesus has waiting for us behind the door of our broken dreams, shattered relationships, wrecked hearts, ruined destinies, and damaged bodies.

God desires you and I to be whole in every way; transformed, anointed, agile, full of vitality, empowered, joy-filled, and rich in abiding faith despite the trials and tribulations we encounter. The treasures we glean from the power of His redemption is ours for the taking. He shares, if we love and obey Him, we will spend the rest of our lives in a state of peace and prosperity. (Job 36: V 11)

Yet, when we think about prosperity, greed-based struggles can at times overtake us. A counter-war occurs inside us breaking down confidence in a God who promises to supply all our needs, versus our self-preservation and ego which strives at all costs to succeed. After all, as scripture describes, it's easier for a camel to pass through the eye of a needle than for a rich man to enter heaven. (Matthew 19: V 24)

How do we responsibly operate as Christians in a world built on the relentless bombardment of "get rich schemes," "I need to survive," and "it's all about me?"

In God's domain, prosperity has little to do with monetary wealth. Rather, spiritual prosperity is marked by divine affluence, favor and anointing from God. It's peace during adversity, contentment, trust and confidence amidst a storm. It is the assurance that all is not only well when it appears to be not, but rock-solid assurance that plans for "good and not evil" are being divinely choreographed behind the scene to assist and restore you. (Jeremiah 29: V 11)

It's spiritual certainty during adversity, anointed healing and resilience during periods of sickness. It's seasonal upswing when the world is on the downswing, poise and grace through endless challenges, and steadfastness and perseverance through tragedies. It's sureness of purpose when the voice inside your head is telling you the opposite; and lastly, the completion of your mission and destiny in life in accordance with God's perfect will for you. These spiritual riches hold priceless benefit for us while we live our lives under the mantel of a fallen world.

God's grace doesn't guarantee the removal of every type suffering in your life. That's where you and I get tripped up. Even though God is the finest sin collector in town who's perfectly capable of saving us from the downpours in life, His favor is not a ticket to a storm-free existence. We reside in a fallen world. Utopia is waiting for us, but not now, not while we're living out life on mother Earth. However, faith is the trigger which brings spiritual providence, internal riches, and His kingdom power which is within you.

Kingdom power is necessary to live a life worthy of the calling. It's continual presence of the Holy Spirit hedging you in, guiding your moves, safe-guarding your whereabouts, transforming and renewing your mind, protecting your space, assisting your circumstances, healing your body, sending godly wisdom, and re-directing you and I from the bad choices we make daily. These spiritual offerings, given to us through grace, empower and refuel our spiritual and physical being daily.

Jesus positioned us on solid footing when He died for us on the cross. He is our spiritual rock. Yet even though our rock of salvation is strong and immovable, we are not. We have a responsibility to ourselves, and to others in our relationship with Him. If we uphold His spiritual boundaries in the context of free will, we glean the abundant life promised, including healing. His simple divine formula works this way:

"Everything is possible for him who believes."
(Mark 9: V 23)

Following Christ is not a free-for-all relationship. Redemption is available, but, authentic relationship with the God of the universe demands— just like any marriage—a mental, physical, and spiritual workout. It requires lathering up a spiritual sweat on the treadmill of life. It presses for high incline, stretching of heart and soul muscles, tripping up and getting up while we live out the Gospel of healing through the frail and fallen saga of our messy lives. Although our minds and hearts require a large portion of spiritual discipline through grace, to reap the benefits of a well-lived life,

God's plan remains foolproof. He gives us everything we need to follow the script.

He desires for each of us to reach our highest spiritual potential, learn the way of love, and recapture our intimate relationship with Him so *we can* experience His abundance of riches. His grace and power are palpable, fresh, and new each day; freely offered, freely given, restoring and repairing us from the inside out, and the outside in.

Although many individuals pray and focus on physical healing which is important to God, it would be shallow of Him to perform only one aspect of healing with the many lists we organize before His throne. He desires to transform the entire house and rebuild us from the ground up. This requires divine remodeling on His part, and a large measure of courage, faith, fortitude, perseverance, and yielding on our part.

The first step is willingness to unlock the door and step into the mess. Some houses require heavy-duty cleaning before transformation occurs. Others demand whisking away of hidden cobwebs, removal of dirt under the carpet or industrial-strength sweeping and scouring in hidden corners for change to take hold. Still others, necessitate a touch of light dusting or tidying-up on a periodic basis to ensure heavy dirt hasn't inched its way back in. Some clean-up areas will be time-worn, rundown and familiar, while others will be surface-polished with hidden grime lurking behind doors, and under beds which are out of sight, out of mind. Either way, any exercise of faith which launches a major spiritual clean-up will most likely leave one fragile, unless we hold tight to God's promises during the walk-through. When internal structures are reformed, spiritual renewing takes place, and accessibility to the fullness of His power is limitless.

Deliverance from the old to the new, from the familiar (sin) to the unfamiliar (holiness) is the stepping stone to a fresh new start, a rebirth into a newly constructed inner home that is bright, redeemed, and bursting with spiritual treasures. Only His love, power and faithfulness can launch the necessary groundwork to enter this state of healing, repair, and renewed relationship with Him that will change your life and reroute you in a whole new direction. Once the foundation is set, the physical body follows suit, wholly reconciled to the spirit, and functionally restored to live out a destiny that serves His plans and purposes.

His Promise of Healing is Yours!

CHAPTER ONE

Understanding the Nature and Power of God for Breakthrough in Your Life

We live in a fallen world. There's no way around it. Countless men, women, and children struggle with God's scriptural promises of supernatural, and miraculous healing. Most individuals, many who are Christian, express disappointment with seemingly unanswered prayers related to sickness, life-threatening disease, tragedy, loss, or life-altering events.

They are not alone in their struggles. Neither are you.

What is healing all about, anyway? Why do some individuals experience physical healing or cure while numerous prayers from others seemingly go unanswered? Why do babies die in the womb or are born deformed, while other infants thrive at an early age? How is it that many individuals struggle with life-threatening illness or treatment failure, while countless others breeze through medical interventions, and experience healing, health and vitality? Why are various individual's victims of tragedy or premature death while others live to a ripe old age? How come various men, women or children battle with serious mental illness, while scores are gifted with mental stability, and clarity of mind, living out their lives with confidence and determination? Finally, why do only handfuls experience God's miracles, yet most seemingly do not?

Is this some cruel divine joke meant to confuse us?

Even though we live in a fallen world, God has ultimate authority to heal, intervene, protect, and perform supernatural and miraculous interventions on our behalf. His word is absolute, equipping us with *seven rock-solid kingdom principles* which guarantee His divine power to faithfully act on our behalf.

With over thirty-eight years of professional practice with physical and mental disease, death and dying in the healthcare field, and my own encounter with a so-called incurable illness, of one thing I am completely certain. *We have a loving, powerful, faithful God who deeply cares, and wants to heal us.* This is the ultimate will of God for His children individually and collectively. So why does it appear that sometimes He does not care?

Gods Nature

The book of Genesis introduces God to its first readers, and shares about His astonishing ability to create and bring forth life. His power not only designs inanimate life; it constructs animal life, mammal life, vegetable life, and human life, while conjoining millions of solar systems around an endless array of clustering stars that outnumber the grains of sand on the Earth.

If you're searching for an unshakable reason to validate God's ability to heal, rebuild, restore, renew or protect you, take my word for it, you're in the best position to have your prayers answered. His power to sustain, and guard you against bodily and spiritual harm, is equal to His immense power to create an entire cosmos simply through the power of His word.

Sometimes, God chooses to perform supernaturally in impossible situations so His glory will manifest in an undeniable way. These powerful signs are faith builders which display His resplendent power. There are countless witnesses from the early Church right through to today, who testify to the supernatural and miraculous power of God. These glorious experiences cause wonder, marvel, and deepening of our faith and relationship with Him.

He also intervenes or works through the healing gifts of others, so we can harness Godly support, and gain vital spiritual lessons. These spiritual trainings prepare us for battle through ordinary and extraordinary interventions, bring wisdom in front-line warring, ratify trust, and help us gain confidence in our relationship with Him.

Lastly, on occasion, God says "No" to our prayers. His "No" is an actual "Yes" if you trust His answer through the eyes of faith. He always acts within our best interests and ultimately works all things together for good to accomplish His divine purposes. (Romans 8: V 28)

The First Principle
Nothing is Impossible with God. His Power is Limitless in Your Life.

God is sovereign over everything. His power is unstoppable, immovable, and unshakable. He cannot be swayed, detained or swindled from the perfect plans or purposes He has for you, ever.

If you long to understand God, and His immeasurable ability to perform, create, fix, heal, or by divine choice intervene in any situation in your life, study Jesus in the scriptures, search the birth of the cosmos or learn about the incredible underpinnings of the galaxy, solar system or wonders of the natural world. His creative power not only formed the entire heavens and universe, but through His divine capability, He also stunningly executes everything He touches with perfect precision, cementing our earthly and eternal blessing.

God nestled our planet in a protective sweet spot in the solar system to sustain life, protect our planet from solar radiation, and disrupt damaging effects from cosmic flares and meteors. Do we call it coincidence that mother Earth is cushioned in-between enormous globes which shield us from the colossal blows of most renegade meteor rocks?

Furthermore, His design of man and woman is exquisite, forming both genders in His image and likeness. We share incredible god-like attributes: splendor, beauty, spiritual embodiment, complexity of body, mind, and spirit (three parts in one God—Father, Son and Holy Spirit, and three parts in us—body, mind, and spirit), along with unique internal governing systems.

Why is it that God became one of His own creative works to display His power, and demonstrate His healing through Jesus in the form of man?

He wanted to connect with us.

He wanted to convey that He understands.

3

He wanted you to know that He identifies with what you're going through.

He sought to redeem us beyond our state of disrepair. He never creates junk and is infinitely affectionate toward His own.

God's blueprint and design of the universe, nature, and man point to God's infinite creative personality. This divine design is the remarkable vehicle He uses to accomplish His flawless purposes.

If you want to appreciate the depth of His genius, study the human body, and its backup systems. Our bodily form, internal organ structure, and blood vessel configuration is so phenomenally structured, it's ludicrous to believe that evolutionary events are solely responsible for the complexity, and level of sophistication in the human body. From a scientific perspective, randomness just doesn't work that way. His Godly workmanship interlinks our human DNA, connecting it with billions of cells in the brain alone, while transmitting information in a split second through multiple layers of our neurons and spinal cord. This information superhighway then, precisely links our internal data system with every cell in our body. Its complex interactions allow us to talk, walk, think, breathe, make decisions, power our heart's engine, and push blood through our circulatory system while feeding nourishment to every organ in our body.

Our human structure is also a well-oiled machine. It contains back-up systems so when one part fails, another compensates, and then helps take over to maintain equilibrium. This internal fortress is skillfully designed to regulate organs by triggering precise, and highly integrated complex sequences while conveying messages that work in sync with chemical responses throughout the body in a way science will never be able to duplicate. Scientists stand in humble amazement at the multiple functions and interactions of the human body, and will remain astonished for centuries to come.

So why is the first kingdom principle about understanding God's powerful nature and ability to heal, necessary? God states,

> "Remember the former things, those of long ago; I am God, and there is no other; I am God, and there is none like me. I make known the end from the beginning, from

ancient times, what is still to come. I say: My purpose will stand, and I will do all that I please."

(Isaiah 46: V 9 - 10)

His presence in our lives, and faith in His ability to heal are vital, and necessary components in physical, spiritual, and mental restoration.

"O Lord my God, I called to you for help and you healed me."

(Psalm 30: V 2)

There are three faith determinants on our part which activate God's divine healing in body, mind, and spirit.

- **Trust.** I will trust and depend on God's ability to intervene and believe He will.

    "God, I desperately need you, and believe in faith you're going to work this out."

- **Praise.** I will praise Him through the events in my life that seek to devastate or discourage me.

    "God, I don't have a clue why you're allowing this circumstance in my life, but I choose to love and praise you through it."

- **Belief.** I will believe that God will intervene in my situation, and I surrender it to Him, despite what my circumstances look like.

    "Lord, I don't get this, but I know you do. I trust this is exactly where you need me to be. I thank you in advance for the outcome. I believe you'll be with me every step of the way, and are working your plans and purposes toward a successful outcome."

We please God when we have faith in His ability to perform. We delight God when we approach Him in a spirit of love and trust, not fear. He is a

God of His word. When we carry the power of this word within us, it is more than enough.

> "Because you have so little faith. I tell you the truth, if you have faith as small as a mustard seed, you can say to this mountain, 'Move from here to there' and it will move. Nothing will be impossible for you."
>
> (Matthew 17: V 20)

Isn't it interesting that Christ chose the mustard seed which is not much bigger than the head of a pin? He set the standard small for us, so we could approach Him in faith without feeling overwhelmed by our spiritual inadequacy.

Seasons and Cycles in the Healing Process

God establishes seasons and cycles with everything He creates. Why is this important to know in relation to healing?

We grow, mature, and age through stages and seasons of succession. To accommodate these cycles, He provides spiritual tools such as scripture, the faith community, and gifts of the Holy Spirit that we can access any time, through any situation for the tearing down, changing, restoring and rebuilding of our lives. From a human standpoint, this requires that we understand His instructions on how the tools work. From a spiritual perspective, it compels us to stay close to the source of His power, *so they can work*.

He also gives us natural and spiritual ability to survive damaging influences from our planet, environment, and flesh. He stockpiled earth with biological plants and foods which help thwart bodily disease. He empowered us with an intellect, so we could understand the mysteries in our world. He placed us in relationship with Him, so we could galvanize divine knowledge to resist spiritual assault and reject sin. We are charged with a lifetime of being wise stewards of all these.

Our ability to avoid sin is contingent on utilizing God-given grace and authority. Exercising human will power alone to overcome our spiritual strongholds is clearly self-defeating, and will always at some point, fail, when we use the sword of human willpower as our primary weapon to strike against the personal demons inside us. Our saving grace and power to resist sin is found through intimacy with God. From this wellspring, flows strength and fortitude fueled by the Holy Spirit. He alone sends spiritual muscle to resist the giants of pride, greed, defiance, disobedience, and other goliaths. Like David, we need only a stone and slingshot to defeat the enemy.

Whether you believe the first kingdom principle about God or not, His power remains readily available to restore, and heal you through every season of your life. When you enter a dark room, you flip the switch to turn the light on. Electricity is readily available to you, but you must activate it. Similarly, when you access God's power, it requires functional participation on your part. It's not a one-way street. You need to be in relationship with Him and position yourself in the mainstream of His presence to benefit from His source of power.

Reliance on God is Divinely Orchestrated

God designed and organized man, and the universe in a dependent, synergistic relationship with each other for a reason and purpose.

His divinely created and ordained organisms and structures interconnect, depend on each other, and interplay with one another in the physical world. There is Godly intent here. First, nothing can boast, neither man nor universe. This spirit of divinely created interdependence between man, living creatures, nature, universe, and the cosmos, requires macro-microcosmic relationships. These connections assert the supremacy of God simply through their interdependent set-up. Nothing has godly power in and of itself. At any given point, each gives birth, connects, grows, evolves, ages, then dies out, attesting to God's dominion over it, and the continuum of His master plan for creation. There will be a new heaven and earth . . . Man will perish yet live . . .

> "I tell you the truth, unless a kernel of wheat falls to the ground and dies, it remains only a single seed. But if it dies, it produces many seeds."
>
> (John 12: V 24)

7

Nothing is absolute, except God.

There is no need then, for God to "maintain" divine control over His creative works. His divine power is a given. He's mathematically constant, and always in divine control. He already knows the outcomes with all things, yet holds back or seemingly waits at times from our earthly perspective, to answer our requests. How is this possible? His divine will manifest's in real time according to our free will, while His divine works remain perfect and timeless under His universal eye in the spiritual realm.

"I am the Lord, the God of all mankind. Is anything too hard for me?"

(Jeremiah 32: V 27)

We are constructed under a limitless divinely interconnected network, a cosmic web endowed by free choice, which is coordinated and structured by the very nature of His DNA. This connection, which we see manifested throughout the entire universe, ultimately mirrors the bond of God the Father with the other parts of Himself in the Trinitarian relationship. There is Jesus His son, who is also God, who represents the Father's magnificent love for us, as well as the Holy Spirit, who represents the very breath and soul of God. This exquisite connection they have with each another (which is separate yet one) in the divine realm, reflects the approach in which God divinely created man, creatures, the cosmos, and their relationship with each other.

His exquisite stamp of ownership allows man, creatures, and worlds propensity to move, interact, and interchange with one another in the splendid supernatural and natural order in which He created them. Humanity has ability to work and interact with the world, environment, and universe without God dictating every move. This spiritual endowment of free will in man, or the state of spiritual and relational constancy, manifests itself in us, and all God's creative works throughout the cosmos and heavens (even with the angels). It is the defining blueprint of our Creator, manifesting the hand of God's perfect love toward us. This part of His nature does not deflect power. It affirms His ultimate sovereignty by offering us the ability to make choices for or against Him.

Freedom of choice then, holds great significance when it comes to the subject of healing, and how it plays a pivotal role in our lives to receive His blessing or block it.

So, when it pertains to healing, whenever we state, "God is always in control," *the answer is yes, and well, no.*

Moreover, scripture emphatically reveals the importance of time, seasons, and cycles with His divine works. We are trussed under an umbrella of divine chapters which support God's heavenly purposes.

> "There is a time for everything, and a season for every
> activity under heaven:
> a time to be born and a time to die,
> a time to plant and a time to uproot,
> a time to kill (*folks, this does not mean a time to murder people, but
> it does mean we can hunt and kill for food, and protect ourselves within
> the confines of governmental laws-authors added comment*) and a time
> to heal,
> a time to tear down and a time to build,
> a time to weep and a time to laugh,
> a time to mourn and a time to dance,
> a time to scatter stones and a time to gather them,
> a time to embrace and a time to refrain,
> a time to search and a time to give up,
> a time to keep and a time to throw away,
> a time to tear and a time to mend,
> a time to be silent and a time to speak,
> a time to love and a time to hate,
> a time for war and a time for peace."
>
> (Ecclesiastes 3: V I - 8)

Beyond Science: Faith

Humans have intrinsic ability to grow and evolve in many ways; physically, spiritually, emotionally, and mentally.

The science of evolution shows us how beautifully God's creation has unfolded since the Earth came into being, revealing the connectedness of all life. People of Christian faith affirm that at a pivotal point in time, God separated man from his apelike ancestors, and breathed an immortal soul into him. Hence, the first man and woman were created to live with God for all eternity. Humanity is forever set apart from the animal kingdom by conscience, reasoning ability, and the amazing capacity to think and make decisions. These distinctions allow us to be in a unique relationship with God. We serve a social Being who created us to connect, and intimately relate to Him. God enjoys and wants contact with us!

Our cognitive and spiritual thumbprint then, differentiates us from plant and animal life for a purpose. Without reasoning and communication, we would be devoid of experience; lack essential connection, be cheated of spiritual requirements necessary for bonding, and remain deeply primal in our contact with Him. Our distinction from other animals and mammalian forms is deliberate from His perspective; it holds our redemptive prize. It validates humanity's inner longings for God, and His divine ability to heal us for our final leap to immortality, never to be separated from Him again. He created us to consciously know, love and serve Him. He *wants us* to come to Him for healing.

God also infused in us, the ability to access the miraculous. Through the authority of His word in scripture, we can confront, cast out, and conquer evil. This power testifies to His authority, and provision for us. We do not lack for healing—it is always available. Our ability to exchange powerful stories of deliverance also bolsters communal faith, and bears witness to our connectedness, and reliance on God through each other.

He also hardwired us to interpret and understand the voice of the Holy Spirit, who we communicate with, through the language of tongues. This form of unblemished interaction between God and man, which is confirmed in scripture, embodies a dialect, untarnished by our cognitive nature. The undisputable voice inside us intercedes before the throne room in a spiritual vernacular that is authentic and pleasing to God. It pleads our requests before Him, under the perfect umbrella of God's will. An individual then anticipates a response through the gift of interpretation individually or collectively through the body of Christ.

He provides physical internal back-up systems, medicine, and the ability through ordinary means to obtain treatment for our bodies when disease or illness strikes. He also empowers us with the commanding and breaking of illness, and the ability to cancel its noxious effects over us in mind, body and spirit.

Satan would have you believe a lie: that you are powerless against forces of the world, flesh, and devil. You need to know that spiritual weapons are available. You are fully equipped and armed to do battle. I will discuss more in-depth about God's power, use of His authority, and the ability to combat forces of evil in later chapters. These spiritual gifts locked away in your treasure box of arsenals include:

1. Calling on the power of His redemptive grace through prayer and the power of His word;
2. Obtaining biblical wisdom for decision making; and
3. Recognizing and avoiding evil through grace;
4. Identifying sin issues through the power of scripture, and the Holy Spirit;
5. Receiving spiritual forewarnings or messages through prophetic dreams;
6. Experiencing deliverance through the authority of His superior blood covenant;
7. Obtaining angelic assistance to warn or protect you from danger (this is scriptural); and
8. Discerning evil spirits, and your ability to identify, smash, and eliminate wicked schemes or plots that aim to crush or destroy your life.

He provides abundant resources for us through the supernatural, miraculous, extraordinary, and even the ordinary. All these sources are provisional channels to assist, protect, and heal us. In addition, these divine and human channels that originate from God's heart and His favor, are important weapons to set us free.

His part in the equation is simple. He empowers and strengthens us through His word, showers us with continual grace, gives us spiritual intelligence through scripture, and infuses us with divine intuition from the Holy Spirit. He keeps us from harm; shelters, protects, shields us, provides refuge, repairs, renews, and sustains us on Earth.

Your part in the equation is also simple. You may not be aware of this, but your heavenly treasure box is teeming with tools. You need to embrace these treasures, arm yourself, activate them, and *respond.*

God always maintains sovereign influence over everything He creates without breaking your free will or God-given right to self-determination. The divine law of agape love doesn't force you to love Him; it invites you to choose Him or, if need-be, permits circumstances to unfold in your life to discover Him. His powerful provisions ensure everything is available to you, so that you can be satisfied in this world, and immeasurably happy in the next. You bear His marking and wear the breast-plate of His spiritual power. This marking gives you access to His spiritual authority, places claim on His promises, and releases physical healing, spiritual saving, mental, and emotional restoring, and unshackling from the strongholds of addiction, sin, and the power of satan.

God's dominion over the universe and His heavenly domain is not all consuming with Him. He's not preoccupied with the need for control like man or wanting to manipulate His creative works on His own behalf. He is GOD. His authority is divinely stable under His permissive will. He has intimate knowledge of everything He has ever created; every era and person who has ever lived, every plant, animal, mammal, star, and planet He's brought into existence. Everything in the universe bears His artistic handprint. Just as a master painter knows every minute detail of his own painting, God knows every detail of His own creation. He exists outside of our earthly dimension of space-time; thus, knows all things, sees all things, has limitless knowledge of past, present, future events, and maintains an all-encompassing loving universal presence. He is not limited by time; everything is present to Him all at once. This allows the magnitude of His divine flow to be available everywhere, in every moment, with all who need it. His divine nature acts completely opposite to Earth's laws and dimensions, yet its influence is divinely pervasive. We, however, are confined to limited understanding due to embodiment in the flesh, which restricts our capacity to fathom the limitless height, breadth, and depth of God's nature.

There's good reason we're confounded when we ponder Him, are puzzled by the vastness of His works, or at times feel baffled or disbelieve He exists. The human mind can't comprehend the fullness and magnitude of God. His divine capacity is magnanimous from a human perspective.

There's no way of measuring His divine presence. He's vast, and totally incomprehensible. That's why God came to us in the form of the God-man Jesus, so we could grasp His nature through our limitations. The people of His day could hug, touch, love on Him, and relate to Him from a purely human perspective. Today, we relate to Jesus through the stories that those who knew Him or knew of Him left for us in the scriptures.

God does provide inklings of the other side. But there's only so much we can visually see or comprehend about the heavens, and spiritual world. We're limited by start, and end points of time that prevent us from fully knowing. There is also good reason His outpouring of mercy and grace is given to us in limitless quantities, despite our inadequate vision, defiance, and self-will. The heart of God is always in a perfect state of love toward us, regardless of what we say, do or think. He is always accessible to us, willing to extend divine assistance, and eager to welcome His never-ending prodigal son's and daughter's back into the fold.

Separation from God

God designed you with free will to act upon your own circumstances. Sin or faithlessness doesn't rustle God's feathers. He's already won the victory over sin and death through His son, Jesus.

Sin issues cause serious impairment in us though, when we willfully separate ourselves from His love and grace through lack of spiritual discipline, carnal activities or poor choices which hurt us or others. These behaviors cause physical, spiritual, mental, and emotional wear and tear, bear gravely on our soul, and can block His spiritual power. This happens not because of Him, but us. When we oppose His grace and power, when we make a conscious decision to separate from Him, our spiritual tanks run half-empty. We obstruct the powerful flow of the Holy Spirit from equipping us, and thwart Godly capacity to be victorious during episodes of physical, spiritual, or mental assault. We need to stay positioned in the mainstream of His grace, so we can maintain God's property—our body, mind and spirit—responsibly.

As co-participants with God and His creative works, our talents and gifts can be used by Him as channels of healing. For example, discoveries and inventions in science, and medicine are approved and knit into the fabric of His heavenly tapestry. These gifts testify to the godly spirit in man, and ultimately acknowledge God as the source of healing.

> "His divine power has given us everything we need for life and godliness through our knowledge of him who called us by his own glory and goodness. Through these he has given us his very great and precious promises, so that through them you may participate in the divine nature and escape the corruption in the world caused by evil desires."
>
> (2 Peter I: V 3 - 4)

In the final analysis, God doesn't need to prove Himself by performing miracles or showcase His power through supernatural events. He is infinitely able to do these and more. He is already superior to every government known to man and holds matchless wisdom to us. Every Godly intervention or withholding by Him serves an all-knowing purpose individually and collectively, which ultimately works for us, and the greater good of mankind. He even uses our flaws, mistakes, and slip-ups to His divine advantage.

If we humbly approach and acknowledge Him as the one true God, He will support, guide, and empower us through every challenge. When we respond to the Holy Spirit, whose nature and wisdom is God Himself, His thoughts and ours meld together. When we take on the mind and spirit of Christ, our choices and decisions reroute in the direction of a higher source. Corrective actions become clear. Thoughts become a mirror image of His eternal wisdom, saturating the deepest recesses of our hearts, empowering us to act. Matthew's gospel shares with us a simple formula on how to discern God's will.

> "But wisdom is proved right by her actions."
>
> (Matthew II: V 19)

This "higher" wisdom places sober responsibility on us when it comes to choosing. We must discern whether our decisions help or harm us, draw us close or far from God. We need to discern whether our choices line-up with scripture, and ultimately bear good fruit. To achieve spiritual and earthly success, we need to fortify our internal fortress with building blocks made of spiritual brick and mortar. These vital ingredients found in scripture, will help us operate like a well-oiled machine. We must also pray for the wisdom of God to fall afresh on us daily!

Often, we deny, overlook or ignore warning signs or symptoms that crop up in our lives. Spiritual warnings, or the spilling-over of high-alert information into our minds from the Holy Spirit, signal us when something is off-kilter. If spiritual, mental or physical forewarnings remain unchecked, or we deafen our ears to the messages they convey, we can leave ourselves wide-open for attack.

Unfortunately, it costs us when we ignore stress, upsetting or obsessive thoughts, give in to self-destructive behavior, or succumb to temptations that hurt others. We can mentally and physically deteriorate when we allow feelings of hopelessness to overcome us, become cynical when we fuel apathetic attitudes, or become paralyzed when fears or phobias overtake us.

When we yield to anxiety, addictions or compulsions, fuel cycles of insomnia, depression, anger, or rage, jealously, outrage, or entertain notions of hostility or "pay-back with others," we open ourselves up to serious sin. Carrying out any acts of violence (in thought, word or deed) in the name of wrath, ultimately poisons "us" and others against the power of God's light and love. Finally, when we become overly suspicious, paranoid, have distorted, or delusional thoughts we open the door to severe mental illness.

When we're poor stewards of our bodies or deny the body's internal signals, dis-ease happens; chest pains, high blood pressure, headaches, migraines, bodily aches and pains, fevers, weight gain, weight loss, poor dentation, high or low blood sugar, cycles of gluttony, morbid obesity, anorexia, hip, bone, knee, shoulder pain, infections, broken bones, limb swelling, tumors of every kind, fatigue, breathing difficulties, and other serious diseases and ailments that indicate our body is in trouble. Often, procrastination, denial, or lack of spiritual wisdom prevents us from getting help.

Truth is, our body, mind, and spirit were created and designed by God, with a built-in mechanism, to alert us of imbalance with our physical nature. We must courageously act and put aside procrastinating when forewarnings appear.

> *"I don't feel good. I need to pray and seek Christ's wisdom and direction. These ominous signs are telling me something may be wrong." "I need to seek medical attention."*

Scripture shares,

> "Do not conform any longer to the pattern of this world,
> but be transformed by the renewing of your mind. Then
> you will be able to test and approve what God's will is—his
> good, pleasing and perfect will."
>
> (Romans 12: V 2)

The battleground is in the mind. Satan can enter through your intellect or emotions, and influence your spirit, trick, persuade, deceive, create doubt, convince, manipulate or tempt you. We can access God's power to handle these onslaughts of the mind and spirit because Jesus gave us His power, and tells us irrevocably, *we can.*

> "I can do everything through him who gives me strength."
>
> (Philippians 4: V 13)

This spiritual and experiential framework which we read about in Philippians, not only encourages us; it bolsters our physical and mental reserve, and sets the underpinning for a type relationship completely dependent on God which is loving, beneficial, and creates a healing partnership rooted in His power. This connection remains active throughout our lifetime if we remain steadfast in a posture of prayer, praise, repentance, and forgiveness. His word then, in scripture, is a double-edged sword that cuts deep into the spiritual and physical marrow in each of us: redeeming, restoring, renewing, strengthening, and rebirthing us while exposing pride, resistance, disbelief, sin, and rebellion.

Let us Pray

Dear Lord,

As I come into Your presence, I want to thank and praise You for the wonders of the universe, the creation of man and woman, and Your blessings upon the earth. I acknowledge the provisions You've made available for me to help defend and protect me from illness, evil, and the trials and tribulations of this world.

As I begin this journey, I want to reconnect with You in new and exciting ways. I desire for You to free me. I want to live life to the fullest, just as You've promised in Your word. I desire to be liberated from the shackles of sin, flesh, and the devil which seeks to rob me of a life-giving relationship with You, and deter my spiritual, and earthly destiny.

I ask You to forgive me for anything I have done in thought, word, or deed which has separated me from having an unwavering relationship with You.

Please reign Your healing power over me, and begin a rebirth in my body, mind, and spirit. I ask to receive all the benefits You have for me through the gift of salvation so that I may live a life worthy of Your calling.

Thank You, Father. It is in the name of Your son Jesus I pray. Amen

CHAPTER TWO

God's Healing is Perfect in Your Circumstance

Why do some people experience healing while other prayers seemingly go unanswered? Do we serve an unfair God?

After working over three decades between the hospital, psychiatric, and ministry settings, I discovered no two patients were alike in their approach to illness or personal journey of healing, even when both had a similar diagnosis. I also noticed prayers of faith for the sick hastened healing, and restored bodies more quickly, while limited faith or absence of spiritual support yielded somewhat poorer outcomes, and seemingly higher mortality rates. Those who relied on their own limited human reserve seemed to experience greater emotional strife, and physical exhaustion from attempting to solve things on their own power. Those who had simplistic faith, relied on God with strong belief in His ability to heal, were divinely bolstered through their difficulties, often reaping seemingly shorter recuperation periods, and improved outcomes.

The Second Principle

God answers every prayer of yours for healing. He is perfect and cannot make a mistake.

A story illustrating the second principle occurred when I was serving the medical-spiritual needs of villagers in a remote village in West Africa with limited food, water, and medications. One man who stood on the service team's "care" line had a leg ulcer which was filthy, packed with mud, and oozing infectious pus that smelled foul. The wound was rotten, gouging into superficial parts of the muscle. The only supplies that remained were a small jar of silvadene cream (which contained sulfur compounds for inflammation best used on burns), and some gauze wrap with a few four-by-four sterile dressings. We served hundreds of men, women, and children that day. Most of the supplies were exhausted by the time he stepped forward to be treated. I knew for all intents and purposes that the wound would never heal. Without constant wound-care diligence, medication, and attention the ulcerative opening was doomed to get worse, especially due to the limited care he would receive, and the medically-deprived environment he lived in. It also seemed certain that this unfortunate villager would soon succumb to a serious blood infection.

However, I understood the biblical foundations of God's power to heal and restore this hopeless situation, and firmly believed a miracle for this humble man. I cleansed the wound with clean fresh water from a tarnished water pump in the center of the village, wrapped the wound with fresh gauze after placing a small amount of the cream on top and around the upper crevices of the opening, and packed it with dry four-by-four sterile dressings. I instructed the man to keep the wound as clean as possible, left him with the rest of our meager supplies, trained him on how to care for his leg then asked God to do what He does best. I prayed over the hole in his leg, pleading for Jesus to restore the ulcer for His honor and glory, and do for the man what he could not do for himself: *give him a miracle, and restore his leg to the fullness of health as a testament to God's power, and as a witness to the other villagers.*

Fast forward to one year later, when I returned to the African village to follow-up with the men, women, and children treated the previous year. I'll never forget walking past the familiar grass huts when the village leader approached me and pointed to the man with the severe leg ulcer whom I had treated the year prior.

"Do you remember him?" he questioned.

Honestly, I did not. The man to whom he was pointing was lean, young looking, and tall. He also appeared healthy, and in good physical condition.

"No, I don't. Who is he"? I reluctantly asked.

"He's the man you treated and prayed for a year ago with the hole in his leg," as the village leader replied he clutched my arm and yanked me toward him.

I gasped, recognizing his ear-to-ear grin once the man caught sight of me.

The village leader sternly commanded, "Show her your leg!" as we edged in closer.

When he jerked his ripped pants above the right knee, the ulcerative hole was gone. In its place was a barely noticeable, thin scar. Chills ran up and down my spine. We got our miracle! He not only received a physical healing which served as a testimony to the other villagers, but experienced a deepening relationship with Jesus which yielded tremendous blessings for him, and the men, women, and children in the village.

Welcome to God's method of healing, and the distribution of His redemptive power beyond all odds!

Two Levels of Healing

God's plan for us to experience healing or cure operates on two levels. The first level relates to God's ultimate will for all humankind. He ultimately created us to live in perfection with Him through plan 'A' in the Garden of Eden: sin free, disease free, and spiritually devoid of evil attacks so we could enjoy a perfect relationship with Him.

On a human scale, we still experience this plan in the spirit of faith and hope. Circumstances have obviously changed because of the fall of Adam and Eve. For example, we will live in a state of perfection, and immortality with Him *after* we physically depart from earth. We will experience bodily perfection completely free from *all* disease *after* we die, when we live out eternity in our final resurrected bodies. This is our total healing. Therefore, we still have access to His ultimate will for us, but timing and circumstances have shifted.

The second level of healing works through the permissive or conditional will of God in our fallen world to repair, and restore our body, mind, and spirit despite our sinful nature. Jesus's sacrifice on the cross launched a spiritual revolution of redemption and healing, but sin and human decisions dictate how this intervention is going to play out. God is not to blame for your troubles or mine. Influences from the world, flesh, and devil trigger spiritual strongholds which can limit God's benefits not because of Him, but because of our resistance toward Him which can block His flow of healing.

Nevertheless, God's permissive or conditional will is just as powerful as His ultimate will for us. They are on equal footing. His permissive will acknowledges the messiness in our lives, self-centered decisions, and sin. Yet His redeeming power to forgive, and emancipate us from sickness in body, mind, and spirit is still available to us.

God also allows situations to unfold in our lives in keeping with our own will about matters, without interfering, often to enhance our spiritual growth, and relationship with Him.

His blood covenant with us then, encompasses three-fold results:

1. It covers our body, mind, and spirit.
2. It positions us with access to heaven through a forgiven relationship with Him.
3. It sets us up for continuous healing and restoration.

God is perfect. He knows exactly how to answer your prayer in keeping with His great love for you. You may not always understand His answer or timing regarding a request for healing, but your faith is the delivery system which assures without question, that He is acting perfectly on your behalf. This means at times He may seemingly answer "No" for your own spiritual protection, have a greater purpose in mind for your spiritual well-being, or delay a response to your prayer to divinely orchestrate nobler circumstances. He may even use your situation to strengthen your character, and spiritual relationship with Him. Sometimes, the outcome can indicate your time, finished purpose, and spiritual destiny on earth is complete.

You may not want to hear this, and neither did I when I was initially diagnosed with the big "C," but release from the flesh is not only a transition, it's the ultimate form of final and perfect healing we're promised as His children. No one can escape physical death. However, we celebrate death just as we honor life. We have resurrection! We have victory through Christ, which enables us as mortals to live in a spiritually transformed state of immortality where illness and disease is completely absent.

"Where, O death, is your victory?
"Where, O death, is your sting?"
(I Corinthians 15: V 55 - 57)

In the final analysis, His exclusive blood sacrifice places claim on His restorative power to heal you and allows access to all His associated benefits. It also permits you to use His authority as a powerful weapon to break strongholds, and smash demonic influences which deter you from the intended will and plan of God for your life.

God is intentional with healing your physical body but is most attentive to the spiritual condition of your soul. Does this make sense? Your physical body is temporary. It is specifically crafted to hold, protect, and sheathe your spiritual body until you return home. God cares about your physical state of being, and desires to heal it. However, in the final analysis, the body is purposely corrupt, and will die, decompose, and return to the Earth. The health of the soul, and spirit determines our eternal (final) destination.

When God's power is operational, His blood-covenant and healing authority expresses itself through three levels:

1. the Holy Spirit of God, based on (*supernatural power*) or direct intervention from God the Father, confirmed through scripture;
2. the Church, through the prayerful people of God (*miraculous power*), derived from intercessory intervention, and the power of prayer under the authority of His superior blood covenant; and
3. the medical and scientific community, a reflection of God's non-interference with man's right to self-determination and free will (*extraordinary and ordinary intervention*).

These three paths listed from greatest to least, are God's channels to deliver us from spiritual, mental, emotional, and physical illness, both self-inflicted or inflicted by others.

Many contemporary Christians believe God performed supernatural interventions in the early Church solely to promote the Good News, but that this same type healing power is not available to us today.

I disagree with this religious viewpoint. Further, scripture does not confirm this interpretation. This ideology subtly limits the power and supremacy of God. It denies His supreme ability to act in accordance with His own timeless nature, limiting His all-encompassing ability to rescue those He loves. He continues to shower healing on those who cry out to Him today just as they did two-thousand years ago. We can limit or block His supernatural and miraculous interventions or capacity to receive them, through serious sin, disbelief, or mortal influences from the world, flesh or devil.

God, and His manifestation to us in the flesh through Jesus, is the same yesterday, today, and tomorrow. His power is consistent and unchanging. Jesus's dual nature as God, and man enabled Him to exist in our world and His. (Philippians 2: V 6 – 11)

He was in our dimension by choice, yet outside space and time all at once (fully human-fully divine). He was also unencumbered by constraints as God, yet completely human in form without sin, likened to the way you and I live. We embody a mortal nature which sanctions time and space as a limited, once only experience. After death, though, our extended existence has no beginning, and no end because we share the same unconstrained timeless dimension with God through the gift of immortality in His eternal presence. There is no need for us to return, as some philosophies and religions imply. This ideology of thought suggests that God's power is limited. It subtly denies the power of Jesus's death and resurrection. It's a cunning persuasion introduced to man from the spiritual underworld, that disavows the sovereignty, and power of God to fully emancipate, and deliver us from "death" through His son Jesus.

Jesus paid our penalty in full. This means we do not have to revisit mother Earth to repay spiritual debt from prior lives. We are forgiven once and for all. The ransom was paid in full through His son, and scripture does not verify or endorse the phenomenon of reincarnation.

He shares with us in His word:

"... I AM WHO I AM."
(Exodus 3: V 14)

Therefore, what Christ, God in the flesh, promised two-thousand years ago, was not just for an ancient time, geographical location, specific culture, the people of Jerusalem, a particular setting or historical time. It was for all time, all ages, and all peoples, for all eternity! Even though He took on our flesh nature at a precise time in history, this did not restrict His miraculous ability to heal, and transform us throughout time. He entered our world in a sinless state with supernatural ability to embrace both full humanity, and full divinity. This sovereign ability to heal and restore His people during His time on earth as God, while participating in the duality of a timeless existence, *makes it possible for Him to directly restore and heal you today.*

If you don't have an active healing ministry in your Church, or consistently offer prayer, healing, or include the gift of prophecy in your worship community, you are limiting God's power, the manifestation of His healing, and grieving His Holy Spirit. This activity is not only a vital witness to God's sovereignty throughout biblical history through present day, but a living declaration to the world which bears witness to the existence and powerful nature of God, and His authority to intervene with our unique needs. We are in relationship with a God who not only wants to be known, but show His power, and glory simply because He is God.

Some religious communities may avoid prayers for healing during their religious services. They may fear these type meetings might create sensationalism or cause a loss of control over their church members. Or, ministerial groups may lack experience with handling supernatural manifestations or miracles from God when He powerfully moves among His people to answer their specific requests. Prayer and fasting before, during, and after planned healing services not only help confirm God's healing power as authentic but provide grounding, wisdom, and guidance for leaders in the Church. Services protected through fortification of prayer always bring undeniable witness to the existence of God above the frail efforts of man. Whenever we start limiting God's power or pick and choose specific healing gifts over others in any faith-based Christian community, we are limiting the Church's ability to be a fully effective, power-packed witness to the power of Christ. Regular services are effective, but anointing is limited. Thus, lack of healing services based on unspoken fears or quiet insecurity of clergy, ministry leaders, ministers or pastors, restrict the Holy Spirit's healing gifts. While it is vital for Church communities to have structure and process, absence of miracles in a fully functional, thriving Christian church, is a sign that the presence of legalism is blocking to some degree, the ability of the Church to rise-up, receive, and use the fullness of God's power and authority.

Jesus spoke strongly against legalism, rigid rituals and rules, and the disbelief in His ability to perform supernaturally or through man with miracles. For precisely such attitudes He condemned the Pharisees in the early Church community. Churches that thrive under the "anointing of Christ" draw increased numbers, produce the fruits of the Holy Spirit, have increased conversions, growth in Church numbers, baptisms, a surge of compassionate works, a rise in healings, prophecy, supernatural events, miracles, extraordinary interventions from God, and an abundance of teachers, preachers, ministries, and lay ministers in the life of the congregation. Anytime these well-rounded signs dwindle, it indicates that those in authority are headed down a path contrary to the healing purposes of God. It requires Church leaders humble themselves, re-evaluate, pray, fast, and seek guidance to restructure their services under the guidance of the Holy Spirit and scripture, to include these gifts, so that God can act within the fullness of His nature *through the openness and faith of His people.*

> "He called his twelve disciples to him and gave them authority to drive out evil spirits and to heal every disease and sickness."
>
> (Matthew 10: V 1)

Does this discussion about supernatural events, miracles and healing seem far-fetched?

Not at all. After all, He is God, and this is His business, so to speak. It makes perfect sense. Indeed, we have plenty of history with Him when it comes to miracles and healing.

Abraham and Sarah bore a son in their very old age, just as it was foretold. Jonah spent three days in the belly of a whale and lived. Jesus raised Lazarus from the dead. Christ miraculously cured a leper. A child was dead, then returned to life after Jesus touched her forehead. A blind man recovered his vision when Jesus laid hands on him. A demon-possessed man experienced complete deliverance from multiple demonic entities when Jesus commanded the evil spirits out of him, only to enter a herd of swine, and drown themselves in the sea. A woman was instantly healed of a chronic bleeding issue when she touched the hem of Jesus's garment. The Apostles were boating on the Sea of Galilee with Jesus when a raging storm appeared out of nowhere. He stopped the huge squall and calmed the violent waters *just by his word.*

> "The men were amazed and asked, "What kind of man is this? Even the winds and the waves obey him!"
> (Matthew 8: V 27)

When one of the men in the crowd severed a Roman guard's ear when soldiers came to arrest Jesus, He touched the ear with His hand, and instantly restored it. He then rebuked the man stating:

> "Put your sword back in its place," Jesus said to him, "for all who draw the sword, will die by the sword."
> (Matthew 26: V 52)

My heart leaps for joy when I hear stories about Jesus, and His supernatural, and miraculous ability to heal, protect, and save his children. Why? Because we are all privy to the same divine intervention!

Our weakness, dependency on Him, and mustard seed of faith is the actual trigger which petitions Christ's power, and supernatural ability to act on our behalf. This is the living, breathing, flawless power of God, made manifest in us through His son Jesus. He loves it!

Over one-hundred bible verses refer to God's healing. There are over three-hundred statements, declaring, "Do not fear." In the New Testament, we have solid evidence, and numerous testimonies from the sick showing Jesus's power to heal all sorts of infirmities and situations: sin, blindness, hemorrhage, paralysis, deafness, leprosy, seizures, dumbness, fevers, demonic possession, violence, danger, restoration of dead organs, and restoring physical life after death.

The most profound example of Christ's supernatural healing power was His own resurrection after lying dead for three days in a tomb. This proved His divinity, confirming He was God. It would be difficult to provide supporting proof, that the large numbers of individuals who testified that they saw Him after His death, were all delusional. Additionally, it would be statistically impossible to demonstrate that hundreds upon hundreds of people who did see Him after His death, were all misinformed, lying, or contrived the "exact" same story from different areas in that region. Even further, it would be quantitively ridiculous that they all secretly corroborated and matched the precise details of their conversations, and activity with Him *after* His death (due to mass hallucinations). The chances of this happening are near impossible.

In Matthew's gospel, we learn that Jesus went about healing every disease, and sickness in accordance with His will for each of the lives He saved. He compassionately healed those who approached Him with physical, emotional, mental or spiritual disease. His miraculous power restored minds and bodies, infused hope, and gave His Father ultimate glory. *However, we've also learned through scripture that there were some towns He entered where He could not work miracles due to the lack of faith on the part of the people.*

Why?

Simply because our faith and relationship with God the Father, and His son Jesus is the connection which continually bears witness to His power. If you will turn your heart toward Him, you'll place yourself in the mainstream of His healing promises and provisions.

> "Which of you fathers, if your son asks for a fish, will give him a snake instead?" Or if he asks for an egg, will give him a scorpion?"
>
> (Luke 11: V 11 - 12)

Considering our mess-up, God deserves endless credit for the alternate plan of redemption for mankind through the death of His son Jesus on the cross. His priceless sacrifice grants endless wellsprings of physical and spiritual relief uniquely made for you. We can access His power by claiming these truths.

> "I can do everything through him who gives me strength."
>
> (Philippians 4: V 13)

I can do everything through Him, because I have placed myself in the mainstream of His power through grace.

". . . for I am the Lord, who heals you"

(Exodus 15: V 26)

I can overcome any obstacle in my life because of God, whose ability is infinitely greater than mine.

"Do not be like them, for your Father knows exactly what you need before you ask him."

(Matthew 6: V 8)

God cannot fail me. His promises are absolute, and part of His divine nature and personality. He knows exactly what I need and will always act perfectly on my behalf. If He allows natural course of events to unfold in my life that seem contrary to His word or my requests, I will stay in faith, and believe His word above the voice of the world. These experiences are learning opportunities for me that He permits for a greater purpose.

"All these blessings will come upon you and accompany you if you obey the Lord your God: "

(Deuteronomy 28: V 2)

God does not viciously punish me with disease, violent acts of nature or withhold His healing. I am now redeemed from the curse. However, my fallen nature does involve free will which can bear consequences outside the intended will and plan of God for my life.

We learn that health and wealth are rewards of obedience to God. When we are in relationship with Him, we receive the fullness of grace, the outpouring of His Holy Spirit, and divine benefits from His promises. He does not interfere with our decision to reject or turn away from Him. Still, willful decisions which separate us from a state of grace, can place us in harm's way or compromise our health and spiritual well-being.

"Carefully follow the terms of this covenant, so that you may prosper in everything you do."

(Deuteronomy 29: V 9)

My health and healing will flow from having a relationship with God.

> "He who dwells in the shelter of the Most High will rest in the shadow of the Almighty. I will say of the Lord, "He is my refuge and my fortress, my God, in whom I trust."
>
> (Psalm 91: V 1)

I am safe in the arms of my Savior.

Expectant faith is an important key that unlocks God's healing designed in accordance with His perfect will for your life. This is not a cult idea, new age philosophy or some crazy rant endorsing a gospel of prosperity. These promises are hard-core, scripturally-based facts. As God's children, we not only experience the sufferings of the world, temptations of the flesh, and interference from the devil. We have access to healing and restoration from the greatest blood sacrifice made known to man though His son, Jesus Christ.

Let us Pray

Father,

I praise You and thank You for being such a powerful and loving God, and for acting on my behalf even when I do not understand the plans and purposes for my life. Thank You for your Holy Spirit who brings truth to my soul, direction, and wisdom to my mind, health to my body, and life to my spirit.

Give me unshakable faith to believe in Your power to heal me. Help me begin a journey of restoration in body, mind, and spirit. Deliver me from the brokenness inside me and knit me back together from the inside out, and the outside in, so that I may be abundantly happy in this life, and ultimately satisfied in the next.

I believe in faith, that You have unwavering ability to heal me in body, mind, and spirit just as You promised; through the supernatural, miraculous, extraordinary, and ordinary events of my life. Let it manifest in me, according to the circumstances in my life, and Your perfect will for my future.

I trust You will work everything for my highest good, and I wait in expectant hope for the fulfillment of your promise. I trust You and love You.

It is in Your name Father, and the name of Your son Jesus, I pray. Amen.

Do you believe your mountains will move? Let the miracles begin.

CHAPTER THREE

"In the Name of Jesus of Nazareth, Be Healed!"

The Third Principle

God's power and authority works through the supernatural, miraculous, extraordinary and ordinary circumstances in your life. His authority also empowers you, as a Christ follower, to speak healing, and deliverance to yourself and others.

Countless stories exist which testify to God's supernatural ability.

In one book, *To Heaven and Back*, author Mary Neal M.D., shares about her experience as a woman physician-orthopedic surgeon who drowned while kayaking in South America. She describes her out-of-body experience after she was pinned upside down beneath a forceful current. As she struggled to release herself, the small boat remained trapped underneath the river rock while the kayak team frantically tried to free her. After she lost consciousness, a blanket of peace enveloped her as she saw herself dead underneath the water. She traveled from the scene of the accident in her spiritual body, encountering the overwhelming love and presence of God. Following her divine meeting, she was given directions to return to Earth. After being submerged for a period that normally causes brain death, she was revived by the kayak team, and her recovery was deemed a medical miracle.

Harvard Neurosurgeon, Eben Alexander, in his book, *Proof of Heaven*, tells how he contracted bacterial brain meningitis. For days, his body lay in a deep coma while his neocortex shutdown. Physicians worked frantically to save his life by pouring huge amounts of antibiotics into him to combat the massive brain infection, even though his brain showed minimal or no signs of activity. After seven days, he suddenly awakened from his coma, fully alert and healed, and able to describe his experience of heaven. As an initial non-believer and skeptic about the afterlife, he emerged from this remarkable experience with a newfound belief in God.

More than two decades ago, I witnessed a medical team attempt to resuscitate a person in cardiac and respiratory arrest. The individual was declared dead. The doctor shared with the family that the team had done everything they could to revive the patient to no avail. While the health team prepared the body post-mortem, the patient began to breathe; vital signs reemerged, and a steady but slow heartbeat reappeared. The individual reawakened. The patient was later discharged from the medical facility after experiencing true physical death.

Why do these experiences of resuscitation differ from person to person, yet all have overwhelming consistency of having conscious contact with a loving God or an experience of His remarkable power? Jesus shared;

> "In my Father's house are many rooms; if it were not so, I would have told you. I am going there to prepare a place for you."
>
> (John 14: V 2)

He knows the deepest recesses of our heart, the things we love, and the spiritual experiences that bring us joy. It's the nature of God to create deeply satisfying experiences that are unique to each of us. He is also a God of divine design and purpose, who knows the very hairs on our head, and the divine encounters that will fortify, uplift, encourage, and restore us.

Further Examples of Healing

While I was serving on a mission in Africa, a frantic young mother placed a three-week old infant in my arms, stating that the baby had not opened her eyes since birth, even though the mother had made multiple attempts to do so.

I held the child in my arms, placed my hands over her closed eyes, and prayed for Jesus to heal her. I commanded her eyes to open under the authority of Christ. Suddenly, to the stunned reaction of the mother, the infant opened her eyes. The creases of her eyes began to ooze small amounts of green pus. After cleansing both eyes with clean fresh water, the baby was fully alert, and smiling after she was returned to her mother's arms.

A woman was diagnosed with a genetic-based, incurable form of cancer. After prayers from her Church community, anointing by elders of the Church, and oncological treatment, she is alive, well, and in remission years later to complete the spiritual destiny God has for her life. Guess who the woman is?

How do we access the unique promises and provisions tailored-made for each of us?

Begin with a relationship with Jesus. God is not looking for you to be perfect. That is impossible. He is not looking for you to prove yourself to Him through good works. You cannot buy your way into heaven.

Bring your wrecked dreams, broken body, hopeless condition, shattered spirit, feelings of inadequacy, worry, and anxiety to His throne. He is more than ready, and able to heal you. He is invincible and knows—as the Divine Physician—the specific course of spiritual and physical intervention you need.

> "Come to me, all you who are weary and burdened, and I will give you rest. Take my yoke upon you and learn from me, for I am gentle and humble in heart, and you will find rest for your souls. For my yoke is easy and my burden is light."
>
> (Matthew 11: V 28 - 30)

Your relationship with Him places you in the mainstream of assurance and faith that God is not only for you, and not against you, but ready to act. In Jeremiah 30: V 17, we learn about God's heart toward us:

> "But I will restore you to health and heal your wounds,' declares the Lord . . ."

His spoken promise, poised on the wings of divine love, is an emphatic pledge that restates time and again: *"You're My Child. Trust Me, I've got this."*

God's Loyalty

God will always show Himself strong on your behalf. He is fiercely loyal, and deeply identifies with your pain through His son Jesus, against the weight of sin in the world.

He carried the full burden of humankind's sin on the cross. He gets it. He can "shoulder it." He's the one person who's walked a mile in your shoes, who completely relates to your set of circumstances.

Even though no one can see the face of God and live, His invisible and seemingly intangible presence is manifest throughout the entire cosmos. This is one reason He presented himself to us in the form of man. Jesus did not only come to save and redeem us. He is a God who wants every part of Himself known to us in every way, for our benefit.

God's Personality in Relation to Healing

The characteristics of God's nature and personality in relation to His ability to heal us then, demonstrates through scripture that He is whole, perfect, protective with those who are His own, can never make a mistake, is universal, immovable, unchangeable, and can never lie.

The way He chooses to heal you reveals a God who is supremely connected, perfected in love, and multi-dimensional in nature. He is a wholly divine spirit, yet embodied with three separate, distinct, communal parts. If this does not tell you that God-in-three-persons has an inherent love for Himself and you, nothing ever will. In fact, God meshes the entire universe together in a connected relationship with Himself, and us, as a mirror image of His divine nature and personality.

If the "one God in three persons" blows your mind, you are not alone. Think of water. It has three natural qualities. Water can be solid (ice), liquid (fluid), or steam (gas). Its properties have inherent changeability, yet even though it can exist in different forms, water will always be water.

Everything He creates is a distinct reflection of His relationship with Himself as God, just like everything you create (in a much lesser capacity), reflects your unique personality. Did you know that God is not only creative but has a sense of humor? Do you think Jesus never enjoyed a light moment with His twelve disciples or never laughed? I cannot imagine Christ being a boring, ultra-serious God who never cracked a smile or enjoyed a belly laugh with His friends during His time on Earth. Scripture shares with us that He was like you and me in every way except sin. He rejoices in our healing, and cries with us in our sorrow. How do I know this?

When Martha approached Jesus, she was angry and upset because Lazarus died. She felt Jesus had let her down because He was absent when Lazarus was sick. When Jesus heard of Lazarus's death, He cried. However, Jesus had a greater plan in mind. Even though He grieved, and wept over the loss of His friend, He purposely delayed His travels to Lazarus' burial tomb.

Why? To reveal the power and glory of His Father to resurrect, restore, and make Lazarus new. He raised Lazarus from the dead after days of bodily decomposition so there would be no question about God's power, and His supernatural ability to bring Lazarus who was dead, back to life.

God the Father is fully revealing to us as much as we can understand Him to be through Jesus. He does not have gender, but for lack of a better word to describe the first person of the Trinity, I refer to God as "He." For all women, remember He made *us* in His image and likeness as well. When we develop in the womb, we're set up with both male and female parts until our genes line up with our chromosomes, and decide under His love, what gender will emerge. We were created not only as a helpmate to man, but to work alongside man in co-partnership with our unique abilities and gifts. He gave us the capacity to bring forth life as a mirror image of Himself, and created us equal to man—separate, yet one. Wouldn't you say this connects us to the mystery of the Trinitarian relationship, and is a testament to our worth as women?

God needs or wants for nothing, unlike each of us. He is sufficient with Himself, and keenly aware of everything you're going through. He knows your prayer requests even before you ask. He also knows your eternal fate.

He is undivided in spirit, never double-minded (while humanity continually wars between the flesh and spirit nature), is incontrovertible, and will never go against Himself. At times, He will intervene for you in ways you will never be able to comprehend. I call him my God of opposites because He always works opposite to the way I think He should or will act. We can limit God or place Him in a mental and emotional box when we do not trust His interventions that materialize in ways that are different from what we expect.

When He does intervene, His actions are perfect despite what we think or perceive. He always intervenes with our best interests in mind because He knows us infinitely better than we know ourselves. He may at times seem *painfully* just, but always acts in accordance with the divine laws of good, in perfect wisdom and absolute truth. This defines the very nature of a just God. He is the only one who is not only perfectly righteous and holy, but divinely acts from a spirit of divine justice and holy vengeance without committing offense or sin against Himself or us.

> "Do not repay anyone evil for evil. Be careful to do what is right in the eyes of everybody."
>
> (Romans 12: V 17)

> "Do not take revenge, my friends, but leave room for God's wrath, for it is written: "It is mine to avenge; I will repay," says the Lord.
>
> (Romans 12: V 19)

He cannot instigate evil plans, conjure up half-truths, physically murder you, viciously strike your life, embody evil intent against you or commit devious acts to destroy you. Since He is perfect, He cannot act against His own supremely good and perfect nature.

Who, then, is the God of the Old Testament?

This question will take another whole book to answer. Simply stated, the God of the Old Testament whom we seemingly do not understand, is the same as the God of the New Testament, revealed to us through Jesus. You are seeing more of His "just" side in the Old Testament because the people of the day were unredeemed, unteachable, and spiritually blinded. They were incessantly committing horrendous acts of evil. Satanic activity was in full-throttle. The people of the time were not only completely taken over by demonic powers, they were operating under a deadly curse of deception. They did not understand the nature of God, embody the power of His Holy Spirit or interpret God's nature or their relationship with Him through the eyes of redemption. Remember, Jesus had not arrived on the scene yet. God used holy and righteous interventions through select men and women to communicate His messages before Jesus arrived. However, the people of that day were completely blind to Godly truth.

In the story of Noah in the Old Testament, God declared that He could not find one decent trait in any man or woman at that time, except for Noah and His family. He commissioned Noah to build an ark. Noah obediently built the large vessel over an extended period, until he was well into old age according to scripture. He persevered with the task despite the jeers and disbelief of those around him. When God commanded Noah to enter the ark, he obeyed. God then sent great floods to purge and cleanse the entire earth.

It is important to understand that before God acts from a spirit of justice, He either sends forewarnings, raises up prophets or empowers men, and women of Godly intent to announce His message before actual judgement occurs. These admonitions allow His children ample time to repent and seek forgiveness.

Conversely, He acts swiftly and mercifully when His children seek help and humble themselves before Him. This is evidenced by his "rescue missions" throughout the course of history. God's power assisted those He loved, and who loved Him, time and again. His righteous faithful interventions in seemingly impossible situations is evidenced in the Old as well as the New Testament.

Just as He saved Noah and his family from the great flood, He parted the Red Sea, so the Israelites could escape the Egyptians who were in pursuit. He physically fed the Israelites manna that rained from the sky on desert terrain. Although this sustained them daily, they were dissatisfied. They were grumpy complainers who constantly questioned God's goodness and faithfulness. They began to worship false gods. Due to their disobedience, and lack of repentance, their travels were prolonged for almost forty years, even though they were geographically close to the land God had promised them.

We live in the wake of the New Testament, where the curse of sin is not imputed against us anymore. Yet, sin or evil *can* play a part in thwarting or delaying the will of God. He cannot go against our free will, willful defiance, ingratitude, or lack of faith in His ability to perform supernatural or miraculous acts of healing.

Jesus paid the full price for our disobedience. We can buck His faithfulness and love, but, there are consequences; just like the bad decisions you and I make, often lead to negative outcomes.

Through His redemption and resurrection, we have spiritual power, life-giving forgiveness, and the spiritual benefits of repair, restoration, healing and renewal. This doesn't mean we are suddenly perfect, never sin or get sick, nor does it mean we live in a perfect utopian bubble after we accept Him as Lord and Savior. It doesn't work that way.

What in fact does it mean?

We are offered redemptive forgiveness. His spiritual plan for us is complete. When we embrace the fullness of that plan, and a new relationship with Him by being born again, His promises are signed, sealed, and delivered. Our rebirth on a heart and spiritual level connects us to Him in a meaningful favor-filled relationship, equipping us with the staying power, and tools we need to live a victorious life, both on a spiritual and physical level.

There are two scriptural truths about God, and our relationship with Him.

1. In the presence of a God with unlimited power, favor, and blessing, we can limit Him (on our part) through free will or the disbelief in His ability to act.
2. When we obediently follow His direction (in faith), we will always reap the reward of divine favor and blessing.

Scripture also teaches us an ageless truth, about the difference between human folly and divine prudence.

> "A simple man believes anything, but a prudent man gives thought to his steps."
>
> (Proverbs 14: V 15)

Under the cloak of divine prudence, we are equipped with stamina, fortitude, recognition of sin, the overcoming of evil, avoidance of danger, and divine positioning. His protective power is given to us in limitless quantities so that we can stay on the straight and narrow, and ultimately bear righteous fruit.

I will never forget the time I was in-between jobs and received an initial call from a company to interview for a position that would require extensive travel, and frequent absence from home. The salary grade for the job was excellent, yet I had a nagging intuition to refuse the position. Excessive time away from home would interfere with my marriage, steal valuable moments from my ministry, and destroy time and attendance I devote to my faith community in Georgia.

The financial offer was tempting, to say the least. After stating I could not meet the travel requirements for the position, another qualified candidate received the job. I agonized another three months (without a paycheck) before the appointed position God had for me materialized. Throughout my payless period, with only small unemployment checks, God took care of me. The math didn't fit; yet despite the circumstances, my husband and I continued to pay our bills on time, while we continued tithing.

The alternate job position that divinely appeared offered a lower salary but supported the balance I sought between my personal and professional life. This position turned out to be an even greater blessing during the period when I received chemotherapy treatments for cancer. The small department, and kind assistance of my colleagues were all part of the miracle God had lined up for me in advance. Thus, my time away from the job (which I was concerned about), did not adversely affect department activities—though it surely would have—if I had taken the prior position.

When I responded to the exorbitant amounts of grace God was pouring into my life to render the right decision, His guidance helped me ultimately align with His will. Giving into the worldly temptation of "going for the gold" could have cost me. Once the sin issues of pride and greed were resolved, it was clear which decision best matched God's perfect will for my life.

Unfortunately, we live in a fallen world. Sin and disobedience can intentionally or unintentionally cause collateral damage, or directly harm us or others. God does not interfere with any willful offense perpetrated against Him by our flesh or sinful nature. However, He is always ready, willing, and able to offer forgiveness, grace, and use our mistakes to restore our connection to Him, and our human family.

> "And we know that in all things God works for the good of those who love him, who have been called according to his purpose."
>
> (Romans 8: V 28)

> "What, then, shall we say in response to this?" "If God is for us, who can be against us?"
>
> (Romans 8: V 31)

God gives us the prescription to live a healthy and happy life through biblical principles. You may never understand the full revelation of His just nature and think,

"God did not intervene in my situation; what is the matter with Him?"

Yet, He is aware of every situation before it happens, and works it out for your highest good, and the good of those around you. You should never blame, curse, reject or turn your back on God because of a tragedy, injustice, diagnosis of a dreaded disease, or when someone you love dies.

"Why did God cause this?"

"Why didn't God save him or her?"

"Why did God allow this to happen?"

The truth of the matter is, God did not cause it. But if it did happen, then God's "silence on the matter" was allowed for a higher purpose. God did not promise us a rose garden or give us the guarantee that we'd never contend with grief, illness, tragedy, or suffering of any kind. What He did say was, that He would never leave us or forsake us. (Deuteronomy 31: V 6)

Jesus Himself prayed to the point of agony in the Garden of Gethsemane over the revelation of His imminent death. He pleaded with God the Father to remove the betrayal and crucifixion He was about to face, while His apostles lay sound asleep nearby. After He experienced the extreme anxiety of having to accept His own demise—to the point of sweating blood, He was arrested then whisked away to be crucified, while His "loyal" and trusted buddies stood nearby as onlookers and did nothing. So, do you think He doesn't understand agony, grief, rejection or betrayal? He was thrown under the bus, too!

Scripture shows us that Jesus always provides a way through or a way out of our circumstance if we believe and trust Him. There will be times when you'll be unaware of the magnitude of His favor in your circumstance, and other times His power will be so evident it will bring you to your knees. Always give thanks through your situation, because if the world, the flesh or the devil brings you to it, His right arm can, and will take you through it.

The Power of Redemptive Words

I will continue to discuss the forces of evil in succeeding chapters. We have weapons to fight principalities and strongholds!

Using the name "Jesus of Nazareth" by calling on His superior blood covenant is a powerful tool that wards off evil, and makes the devil run faster than a speeding bullet!

If you are sick or in a state of ill health, call out:

"In the name of Jesus of Nazareth, by His superior blood covenant and authority, I call forth healing for my condition. By His stripes I am healed. Amen."

If you are struggling with unhealthy, obsessive, or evil thoughts, temptations or unrelenting sin in your life, simply state out loud:

"In the name of Jesus of Nazareth and His superior blood covenant over me, you must cease and desist immediately, satan. I take this thought (temptation, sin) captive and obedient to Christ. I sever its influence in my life, and command it to leave my heart, and mind immediately. I call forth the Holy Spirit to fill me with fortifying grace, and the power to resist your temptation. Amen."

Watch His powerful word of authority command the temptation to immediately disappear!

If you are in a dangerous situation, state:

"In the name of Jesus of Nazareth and His blood covering, I call forth the mighty forces of God's divine protection to eliminate the danger I am in. Shield me under your divine protection, O Lord, and keep me safe under the shelter of your wings. Amen."

I'll never forget the time my Nissan sports car died right in the middle of a road in a high-crime neighborhood when I was living in Connecticut. It was early in the morning, and the deserted street was off the main thoroughfare. I remember feeling anxious that I would not get the assistance I needed, and that I'd arrive late for work. An old-model gray car pulled up behind me filled with six young men. When I apprised them in the rear-view mirror, my spiritual radar informed me they were up to no good. I quickly called on God for His supernatural protection. In my mind's eye, I imagined a seven-foot-tall angel getting out of the front passenger side door of my car, and walking toward their vehicle. As I watched through the rear-view mirror, the men in the car were laughing as one of them jumped out of the car to approach my vehicle. Right at that moment, I prayed the prayer for supernatural help. Suddenly the man looked wide-eyed, ran back into the car, put his seat belt on, locked the car door with the six men in it, and the vehicle sped off around my sports car at top speed! That's what I call divine protection!

When you use the name of Jesus, state it with a steady, certain spirit. Remain contrite and humble, knowing God's power, not yours, is intervening relentlessly on your behalf. These declarations are not meant to be used as a magic bullet, hocus-pocus saying, or trite statement to get what you want. These expressions of faith and favor are powerful tools when used correctly in relationship with Christ, claim His authority, access His power, and immediately activate assistance from the realm of the spirit.

Remember, Christ won the ultimate battle against evil. He will never tempt you beyond your ability to endure, set you up as bait, or allow you to fall into the hands of evil without a way of escape. This is a scriptural promise. He may at times, seem to give you a bit more than you believe you can handle, only to show you that the power of His strength and grace is greater than yours. As His child, you carry spiritual maneuvers to protect you against the enemy who is looking to engage you in spiritual warfare, and take you out in body, mind, and spirit.

There are times when an individual is martyred for their faith or killed through an act of violence; either from evil intent, or a diabolical mistake of another person. These events which are the sacrificial destiny and choice for the select, are for the benefit of many. The violence they choose to suffer or endure in the name of Jesus is rewarded greatly in heaven, as well as used to provide seen, and unseen blessings with others on Earth. (Luke 12: V 4 – 5)

We are spiritually hardwired to recognize good and evil. Evil is cunningly deceptive and strong. However, God's armor through His word is stronger. It is important to equip yourself.

Read the Word. Memorize the Word. Use the Power of His Word.

God's healing does not only bear witness to your physical health. Your soul and spirit are of paramount importance to Him. Under His all-knowing eye, the Holy Spirit works behind the scenes to orchestrate a series of divine arrangements that open spiritual doors no man can shut. Once you walk through the open door He provides, you'll enjoy divine access to His provision. He knows how to take care of you from the inside out and the outside in. Trust His process. It is infinitely greater than yours.

God can never make false promises to you. What He says goes. He has the capability to listen and respond to your prayers, and millions of other prayers at the same time, just in case you were wondering if God was even listening to your request for healing. He is a jealous God; however, the definition of jealousy is not defined in human terms as having an evil component to His personality or being envious or covetous to the point of committing acts of sin or violence against you. It does mean however, that God has exquisite divine ownership over you, and therefore is divinely protective, and infinitely watchful over your life and soul.

There is only one God. He states,

"You shall have no other gods before me"
(Exodus 20: V 3)

There will never be another god like Him. He does not need to compete against other deities, religions, cults, new age movements or false ideologies that seek to disprove He exists, or blatantly oppose His supremacy. Your decision to worship a god-like idol or permit graven images in your life to distract you from having a relationship with Him, won't change the fact that He is the one, and only true God of the universe. He is perfectly complete, whole, and loves to display His glory. This has nothing to do with Him having a brazen ego, unrelenting pride or bouts of grandiosity, the sins you and I struggle with on a frequent basis.

The fundamental deific truth about Him is, He is not only perfect; He knows it. (Exodus 3: V 14) This is crucial in understanding the definition of "divine truth." Everything that comes from God reflects perfect love and justice, which in turn creates perfect order, and divine unity throughout His heavenly domain. Nobody compares or will ever remotely equal His nature.

The definition of God, then, describes the nature and personality of someone who is not only perfect but powerfully complete. He is wholly integrated, divinely aware of His other parts, and lovingly relational with Himself, His children, and all creation. His creative works are integrated and interconnected, which clearly show His magnificent personality, power, ability, and capacity to create, intervene *and heal*.

You are matchless in His eyes, so never compare yourself or your situation with anyone else. He sees you as complete, and forgiven through His son, Jesus. You play a unique role in co-partnership with Him. Your spiritual and human DNA is not only uniquely yours, but your soul and spirit were created exclusively through His, connecting you to Him, and serving as a distinct watermark on your life.

That is how He can say,

> "Indeed, the very hairs of your head are all numbered.
> Don't be afraid; you are worth more than many sparrows."
> (Luke 12: V 7)

You are irreplaceable, fiercely loved, and wonderfully made. No one will ever top His amazing love for you.

Wealth, status, power, ego, sex, money, fame, material possessions, addictions, or placing people on the "throne" are distractions that occupy the heart, and steal attention away from God. These worldly objects of affection are transient, and will always limit our ability to experience lasting joy.

He states,

> "I am the way and the truth and the life. No one comes to
> the Father except through me."
> (John 14: V 6)

I know this is hard to fathom or accept. New age philosophers believe there are many paths to God. While alternate paths may provide fleeting insight or limited spiritual influence for a time, they will never capture or compare to the fullness of God's divine power manifested in you over the long run. Why would God need to compete with any other path? He is not only perfect; He created the ultimate way for us to experience Him through Jesus. Who would want to consider a lesser path, or follow a god who is second fiddle with literally no resurrection power, and no authentic healing capacity? I certainly wouldn't waste my time or effort pursuing a lesser god, golden statue or alternate path, would you?

Although alternative spiritual ideologies may promote pseudo mystical encounters or incite warm fuzzy feelings for a while, these experiences are a false representation of the divine workings of the Holy Spirit. They lack sustaining power, and do not represent a dependable solid relationship with the God of the universe or His righteous, holy, and magnificent power to heal and transform you. There are no other god-like figures in history who have ever displayed His resplendent power as a God-man, or will manifest His divine power or sovereignty in the future, ever.

God's Creative Power

Do you believe that God is tired of manifesting divine excellence on His own behalf? Do you think He's put a cosmic halt on things? If that were so, it would defy His perfect nature and we'd suffer immensely as a result. Scripture confirms this:

> "Behold, I will create new heavens and a new earth. The former things will not be remembered, nor will they come to mind."
>
> (Isaiah 65: V 17)

If God stopped expressing His divine nature, you would never marvel over the fresh wonders of a brand-new world that is promised for you in the future: the creation of a new heaven, new earth, and the astounding establishment of a future world where righteousness will reign, and God's presence will continually manifest His love, and supreme power. The truth is, God clearly shares with us that He will continue to create. I know you find that hard to believe. I find it extremely hard not to believe. He wasn't finished when He created the "first" heavens and earth. Scripture confirms this revelation.

"Then I saw a new heaven and a new earth, for the first heaven and the first earth had passed away, and there was no longer any sea."

(Revelation 21: V 1)

"But in keeping with his promise we are looking forward to a new heaven and a new earth, the home of righteousness."

(2 Peter 3: V 13)

His ability, age, and life span equals infinity. Nothing is impossible for Him. Absolutely nothing. In Isaiah 40: V 28 - 31, we learn that He never faints, gets weary or needs to sleep. So, do you think He has the power to heal you? Absolutely. We are faith building here!

Here is the flipside of the coin: He does not need us for Him to exist, but deeply loves us, and wants us complete and whole for all eternity.

Even though we bear His redemptive mark, and can easily access His power, we still need to be on our spiritual guard. Evil is cunning and deceptive. When you dabble with evil or the powers of darkness, it will cost you. The rise of violence, greed, avarice, injustice, lies, racial discrimination, rape, murder, child and adult molestation, sexual immorality, addictions, wars, false religions, satanism, and perversions of every kind testify to the devious nature of evil, and its pervasiveness in the world. There is a fierce battle going on for man's spirit between the forces of good and evil. Although satan is already defeated, his main objective is to destroy as many souls as he can before the final curtain call.

You and I struggle with sin every day. The power of sin's influence over us can never destroy our soul and spirit if we harness the power of Christ's light within us to resist it. Satan, and band of demonic cohorts must submit to God and ask permission to rustle our feathers or take us out (kill us). Can you imagine? By the way, satan's name will never be capitalized here. He's already lost the battle, so he gets zero credit in this book.

When God allows the evil one to test or tempt you (for example, like He did with His servant Job), He not only has a plan, but a greater purpose in mind for the manifestation of His power and glory, and for our spiritual edification.

Why would the God of the universe allow us to suffer? Why did He allow Abraham, Moses, Job, Mary His mother, His apostles and some of His most beloved and trusted servants to suffer? Why did God allow satan to tempt Jesus directly in the desert? Why did God the Father allow His son Jesus to experience the most excruciating form of torture imaginable? His skin was torn to shreds with a spiked metal strap that ripped and gouged His flesh. He was beaten to a pulp, almost to the point of being unrecognizable. He was bludgeoned repeatedly. He bled profusely. The Roman guards spit on Him, tore His clothes, then hammered rusted stakes through His flesh. They hung Him on a cross while He suffocated to death by being suspended against the weight of His own body, rendering Him unable to push Himself up on the cross or even draw in a breath, while bystanders sneered nearby.

Welcome to my "God of opposites."

The reason God allowed Jesus to suffer and die, and the reason God allows each of us, at times, to walk "through the valley," is to manifest the power of His resurrection. This is, *The Victory Dance of God*. There is always an extraordinary blessing waiting around the corner when He is acting within our best interest. He always has a higher plan in mind.

Job was a righteous, wealthy man who loved God, and was obedient to Him during his lifetime. Job had a spiritual relationship with God. Even though Job obeyed God, he lost his home and processions. His children were all killed. Ugly boils and sores erupted over his face and body. He was totally disfigured. The ultimate blow occurred when Job was disgraced and humiliated by his wife. Satan tried to demoralize, demolish, and destroy him emotionally, mentally, physically, and spiritually. Even though his life was reduced to ashes, Job refused to curse God. Was he discouraged? Yes. Did he put himself down, and wish he could die? Yes. However, because of his unfailing loyalty and faithfulness to God through it all, in the end, God restored Job to a life greater than before. The enemy lost the victory over this man. Job emerged spiritually stronger than ever before. God blessed Job financially, physically, materially, and relationally; with more children, good health, renewed wealth, and long years—because he remained faithful.

When God does the Victory Dance, His moves cannot be beat.

Remember, you are primary on God's list, and always on His mind. In fact, your status with Him is above the angels. He chooses to relate to you through a unique spiritual relationship which is deeply personal, and uniquely designed for you, and Him to connect.

Whether you believe He is God or not is your ultimate choice. His gift of grace will grant you many opportunities during your lifetime to recognize His internal voice from other voices (John 10: V 27), and draw advice, and counsel from His Holy Spirit. But ultimately, it's your choice to have a relationship with Him.

There is one absolute truth when it comes to God. He is ultimately sovereign over everything. The divine buck stops with Him. Finally, He cannot contradict His own divine laws or state of perfection. This means His character is eternally flawless, unchanging, and perfect all the time in every way. Hence, every intervention, grace, healing, or cure is uniquely perfect in His spiritual plan for your life. This is phenomenal news!

In keeping with the first three spiritual principles then:

1. God's love for us is always perfect. However, our behavior can result in prolonged suffering, a delay in God's plan for us, or an unfortunate consequence due to willful separation from Him.
2. God's love always reaps higher blessing than the one we have in mind for ourselves if we stay the course.

We can turn our back on Him, but by doing so, we will bear the natural, physical, environmental or spiritual consequences of the decision.

That is why scripture states;

> "The fear of the Lord is the beginning of wisdom, and knowledge of the Holy One is understanding."
>
> (Proverbs 9 V: 10)

This type of healthy reverence and fear, borne from having a life-giving respect for the God of the universe, marks the underpinnings of authentic spiritual wisdom.

You do have free will to choose or refuse His redeeming love. He will not interfere with your personal decision to deny, resist Him, or assert your need for self-determination. However, you may not experience the fullness of His gifts, or open yourself up to the forces of evil through sinful choice, forfeiting His protection, and spiritual help.

3.   Not all misery and sickness is caused by sin.

Jesus clearly pointed out that not all sickness is the result of personal or generational sin. (John 9: V 1 - 12) Things happen in an imperfect world with imperfect people. Conversely, the devil is not always the cause of your downfall. Sometimes we give him more credit than he deserves.

Our part is simple. Even though you and I live in a fallen world, if you love God, and are in relationship with Him, He will always intercede, and act on your behalf. His all-consuming love is rooted in His absolute, complete, and perfect will for you. It does not require you to feed it, fuel it or perform good works to win it. All He wants is your love and faithfulness. In return, He will do the rest. Trust His love and believe He will work everything for your ultimate good.

Jeremiah 29: V 13 shares with us that when we seek God with all our heart, we will not only find Him, but be found by Him.

4.   God's love is just.

If you *consciously and willfully choose* to reject God, He will give you what you want. He will leave you to the fate of your own self-reliance. Thus, you may bear natural or spiritual consequences based on sinful defiance, and independence from Him if you refuse His grace. Take your cue from the fallen angels, Adam and Eve, and others who have gone down in history before us. It's a losing battle.

You may think,

"Things are okay now, I don't need Him."

This is akin to placing God in the parking lot. Ultimately, if you continue to reject Him, defy, perpetrate, endorse or entertain evil without repentance, you will forfeit grace, and receive exactly what you want. This will cost you eternity.

Scripture shares that complete rejection of God, especially at the end of life will finalize in unimaginable horror. It is the fullness of the word "death." You will be enveloped in an all-consuming dark void of unrelenting emptiness, accompanied by feelings of total despair, terror, and endless torture knowing you missed the cue. You will experience sensations of being burned and scorched by fire, experience perpetual demonic taunting, and an eternity of deep, cold regret from the realization that you made a deadly mistake. (Revelation 21: V 8) You will never enjoy the rewards of love, peace, joy, or the eternal light of His presence. Believe me. You do not want to go this route. It is hell incarnate, and the complete end of you. (Matthew 13: V 50) (Jude I: V 7)

In scripture, Jesus talks about one and only one grievous sin against the Holy Spirit which can never be forgiven. In a sense, this is a mystery. How can there be one offense that will never be forgiven, after all we've discussed about the forgiving nature of God, and the redeeming superior blood covenant of Jesus Christ through His sacrifice on the cross?

I believe, in fact, the unforgivable sin Jesus speaks about gives us deep insight into the divine justice of God's nature and personality. The unforgivable sin is willful defiance or hardening of one's heart against His Holy Spirit. Despite numerous signs, knocks on the door, holy prompts, undying love, release of saving power, and redeeming grace, if we *deliberately* and *knowingly* mock His Spirit, consciously refuse His love as a matter of choice, turn our back on Him, or reject Him, especially after experiencing the fullness of His love; when we die, we are in for one terrifying encounter with the face of evil. Any willful, grievous denying, unrepentant or obstinate separation from the gentle, loving, wise, comforting, redeeming, saving, all-knowing, and loving Holy Spirit of God will bring total separation from Him for all eternity.

The third person of the Holy Trinity is loving, wise, and full of infinite knowledge. The Holy Spirit is the very breath of God's eternal flame, the "salt of the heavens and holy balm of the earth." The Spirit lovingly influences and transforms people, places, and events on our behalf. He also provides divine wisdom, and insight into difficult situations, while summoning the spiritual angelic armies of God to help and assist us when we're in danger.

He knows the exact mind of God in all matters, and intercedes on God's own behalf with Him, and through Him, because He is also God. As the third person of the Trinity, He is not bound to past, present or future either. The breath of the Holy Spirit is in a continual state of "is-ness," meaning that His wisdom, and all-knowing mind is a living extension of a divine continuum joined with the very soul, and heart of God Himself and Christ existing for all eternity. He continually mirrors the divine thoughts of the dual nature of the God-Head. Consequently, the Holy Spirit produces a continual outpouring of grace to us. His unceasing work in our lives provides wisdom and knowledge which helps us overcome difficulties. He intimately grasps the other two parts of God, Jesus and the Father, and stands as the righteous gatekeeper or bridge between the mind and heart of the Father, and Jesus in the Trinitarian relationship. The spirit of God already knows what offense you commit before you do it, and offers you provision, and way out through grace before-hand.

The Holy Spirit also embodies full knowledge of you through the mind and heart of the Father, even before you were expressed in physical form.

> "Before I formed you in the womb, I knew you, before you were born I set you apart; . . ."
>
> (Jeremiah I: V 5)

Therefore, your conscious turning against or willful departure from the Holy Spirit of God as a final decision to separate from Him, permanently severs the relationship with Him. This is due to God's nature of agape love (perfect acceptance of your free will), His holy righteousness, and the nature of His divine justice. It is also why satan, and his evil cohorts who fully rejected the Triune God after existing in His beatific presence, will never experience the joys of heaven again.

Let Us Pray

Father,

I long to hear Your voice, receive Your grace, and respond to Your love through the power of Your Holy Spirit in new, and refreshing ways that open my mind, heart, and spirit. I accept You as my Lord and Savior, and desire that my heart and spirit be born anew. As I continue this journey of healing, with a spirit of repentance before You, send me Your Holy Spirit. Pour Your grace over me, show me the way, light my path. Reveal to me the truth about the condition of my heart, and its attitude toward You through the power of Your Holy Spirit. I pause in a spirit of awe and reverence before You. Search me O Lord. Reveal to me the areas in my life which separate me from having a relationship with You.

I request through the authority of Your blood covenant to reveal, and remove in me, in the name of Jesus, any spirits of pride, arrogance, defiance, unforgiveness, self-condemnation, fear, retribution, lack of confidence, or mistrust in Your nature or word which prevents me from connecting to You. Restore, and make me whole. I need Your tender healing touch, powerful intervention, and unending mercy to renew and restore my soul. I believe when You are in me, I am enough.

Recapture my heart, cleanse my spirit, and illuminate my soul O God! I long to be healed in every way. Reconstruct my heart, and change me from the inside out, and the outside in.

Hear my prayer and answer it in accordance with Your will for my life. I humbly come before you, and wait for You to show Yourself strong on my behalf.

In the name of Jesus of Nazareth, I pray. Amen.

CHAPTER FOUR

God Heals through the Supernatural, Miraculous, Extraordinary and the Ordinary

God loves when we need Him, *because He is God*. This need for Him, in accordance with our faith, activates healing, and releases His power in your life and mine.

God's ability to heal through the supernatural or miraculous is emphatically confirmed in Scripture. It completely aligns with His love and plan of salvation for you.

Furthermore, God does not need us to perform healing. He can perform it directly if He chooses. We have testimonies dating back over two-thousand years ago which demonstrate how God intervened through delayed or immediate intervention through His son Jesus. We see this in the story of Lazarus who died, yet was resurrected from the dead days later, after all likelihood of life was gone. It was also evident in the story of the blind man whose sight was restored instantaneously, simply through a one-time request to be healed. (Luke 18: V 35 - 42) These divine moves of God which act on behalf of His marvelous love and power, always capture the heart, and full attention of God's children.

Before Jesus died, He commissioned the twelve apostles to physically heal, and cast out devils in His name through this direct power. This compelling commission to heal miraculously in the name and authority of Christ, confirmed the set-up of a co-partnership with the Father giving humanity the amazing ability through the Church (people of God), to perform even greater works than Christ Himself.

> "I tell you the truth, anyone who has faith in me will do what I have been doing. He will do even greater things than these, because I am going to the Father.
>
> (John 14: V 12)

Why then, is healing not always generated through the supernatural? Or, why are we not seeing numerous manifestations of miraculous type healings in accordance with the original commission given to the apostles in the early Christian Church? Is it because we lack the faith of a mustard seed? Is it because we don't carry enough believing power? Not necessarily.

The Fourth Principle:

God's healing power will manifest itself through a unique channel (supernaturally, miraculously, extraordinarily, or even through the ordinary), specifically designed for your life.

Our world and circumstances are akin to a lower story that involves original sin. Not its power over us anymore, but the willful choosing of it. Not our repaired and redemptive relationship with God, but our willful disinterestedness with having a relationship with Him.

We not only bear remnants of our original DNA, we harbor the mutated spiritual strands of Adam and Eve. Hence, our spiritual genetics predispose us to a temperament of spiritual independence and rebellion. Even though we embody grace, we still battle the temptations of sin, influences of satan, and weaknesses of the flesh. This is the lower story of humanity played out under the redemptive upper story of God's mighty right hand.

To this end, man's free will, and the divine nature of God's love unfold yet another mystery about His relationship to us with respect to healing:

God's stream of divine assistance and healing is in a constant state of divine flow over us, which is continually present to mend and repair our body, soul, and spirit. God sees us as perfect, and complete through the redemptive eyes of His son Jesus. To this end, there is no withholding or hindering of outflow; all is available to us. However, our defiance or willful separation from God, can deter the fullness of inflow or divine intake on our part.

Healing then, can occur through extraordinary or ordinary means, and still attest to Jesus's power working through us. God uses everything in accordance with His ultimate and circumstantial will for us because of Jesus, both through "spiritually-equipped" man, and "spiritually-unequipped" man.

Let me define spiritually-equipped man. Healing from Christ, expressed through spiritually-equipped man, bears direct influence on the original commission Jesus gave to His apostles. We see the power of the manifestation of miracles through anointed lay apostles, pastors or lay ministers, especially in remote areas of the world, where Christ works through miraculous channels. These events testify to God's power in an irrefutable way. Individuals who receive miracles through this venue are desperate, eager, sick, and hungry for help. They are unmoved by distractions of the world, sophisticated technologies, greed, money or wealth. Their spiritual humility, and utter dependence on God pleases Him. Spiritual channels open due to unbridled faith, great need, and demand for healing. Activated through raw faith, God's power is seen, and experienced in all its fullness. Hence, miracles, and even supernatural events (direct intervention from God) are plentiful. These events testify to the Great Commission which draws thousands of men, women, and children to the Gospel, cultivating life-saving relationships with Christ.

Jesus's precise time of arrival on Earth also speaks irrevocably to the reason why God ultimately chose the time, season, and age to make His entrance into the world. The people of the time were not only desperate to receive a Savior (perfect timing), but His entrance fulfilled every prophecy foretold decades before.

God's Healing though the Ordinary

When "spiritually-unequipped" man works though ordinary means, God is not moved. Men and women elicit healing response through medicine, and attest to the healing of others through discoveries in science.

This does not hurt God's feelings or promote an attack by God to sabotage man's work. God acts through divine providence, coordination and blessing, ordaining outcomes for the overall good of humanity even though we are deeply flawed.

These outcomes benefit others through the spiritual law of multiplication: one sews, another reaps. (John 4: V 37) The Father's nature of perfect love is not vengeful or envious. God remains in a state of perfect love for us, whether man gives Him credit or not.

Ultimately though, nothing of value, worth or good in us ever comes from any other source than God. God's redemptive mark bears light in, around and through us, just as, conversely, we are redeemed from the curse, yet still influenced by it. God's endorsement to heal others through humanity's ordinary means, is supported through grace but usually encompasses a gradient of suffering the recipient may have to endure—not because of God—but due to man's imperfect state.

At times, we may be the victim of the errors or mistakes of others. Any healing through ordinary means (or our lower story), always serves a higher purpose.

Also, at times, God allows flaws, errors or mistakes to directly or indirectly influence our outcomes. If God can, does, and will protect us, why does He allow this?

Who can ever fully understand the mind of God? Our degree of hardship or the way we spiritually handle these unfortunate circumstances can strengthen us for purposes yet unseen, produce durable character or promote a greater witness for others.

Why did Jesus use ordinary means to achieve supernatural results during His earthly time with us? He had the divine power to halt men plotting to kill Him, but He did not. He suffered shockingly at the hands of cruel men who were sinister, taunting, and deeply unsound, yet He allowed them to torture Him. When evil acts of violence were waged against Him, He turned the other cheek, and intentionally forgave His perpetrators. He was then killed after suffering a merciless crucifixion. These actions seemed so futile for a mighty God, didn't they? God could have swooped in, wrapped it all up, and put a stop to the whole episode, but He did not.

This is the spiritual irony of it all. Through His immense suffering and death, their emerged powerful victory, redemption, resurrection, and new life. This blueprint of events suggests God's truest nature. Who could ever understand why the God of the universe ordained a horrific death sentence on Himself under a horrendous set of circumstances, then seemingly set it up to look like "failure."

The plan was brilliant.

He showed us the full assault of our fallen nature pitted against Him to demonstrate our limited nature, and the ability of His divine nature and power to overcome it. God's redemptive plan set into motion the tenets of our faith, through a belief system we would embrace for generations to come through the retelling of His story, and ultimate sacrifice.

God the Father knew Jesus would transcend His circumstance, defy death, open the gates of hell, and provide the eternal means for our redemption and healing. He also knew humanity would never respond to a haughty god, emulate or revere centuries later, a puffed-up, self-righteous king who saved his people through enslavement, cruelty or domination. He didn't hardwire us in this way. He understood how He crafted us and chose the highest form of sacrifice as the tipping point to break through to our hearts. Therefore, humanity will always be part of a fallen world, but through choice, not victim to it. We have the final victory through Jesus with immortality. Here again is *The Victory Dance of God!*

The story of redemption is clear. Retribution and punishment is served. Jesus paid it in full. You are not under the wrath of God. When tragic circumstances or illness strike, you are redeemed from the curse of spiritual death and annihilation. However, you are still under the mantle of a fallen world.

Tragic events, trauma, sickness, and mental suffering are all part of the lower story, and at times, compassionately allowed by Him. They serve to spiritually season us, bring greater dependency on Him, remind us He is with us, deepen our faith relationship, and grow spiritual virtues in us which would not necessarily have occurred under different circumstances. When God works in man through ordinary means, you may not always understand His intervention. You may question His permissive will or struggle with the aftermath. You may even question God's heart toward you. Remember, He is working powerfully behind the scenes with divine intent to glean your relationship with Him and serve your highest good so stay in faith.

During a mission trip to South America many years ago, one of our NFTN (Nurses for the Nations) team member assessed a woman on the care line who was vomiting, dizzy, and could barely hold her head up. The nurse noted that the woman was leaking clear fluid from her nose. Our lead-ICU nurse immediately tested the fluid for sugar which was positive, indicating a spinal fluid leak. It turned out the individual was a victim of abuse. Our team, and international partner was not only able to arrange further testing for the desperate woman, but later transport her to a facility for treatment. Pastoral counseling ensued as a follow-up. The Lord used our medical, nursing team, and international partners as a channel of God's love that spilled over to the entire family, which brought healing and restoration.

God could have instantly intervened on a supernatural basis by promptly curing her, or miraculously healed her through the team, when they initially prayed over her, but He did not. He understood the heart of the victim, and already knew what it would take for physical, spiritual, and relational healing to occur. Circumstances which require healing of more than one person are often the moments when God acts not only for the benefit of one, but for the strengthening, and salvation of many.

Other examples of God's healing through ordinary means include: taking medications for certain physical or mental diseases, successful surgeries to correct or remove diseased organs or mend broken bones, administering life-saving mechanisms for bleeding or chemotherapy-immunological treatments for cancer. The challenging situations we experience in our lower story, allow us to reap invaluable knowledge, fortitude, strength, and a deepening of our relationship with Jesus in the unfolding of His upper story. These interventions are worth their weight in gold, and a form of healing through the mystery of God's divine will for us.

I'll never forget the time a loved-one in our family met with an unfortunate accident after arriving home from her routine activities for the day. She attempted to park her car in a designated spot near the entrance-way to her apartment complex. After getting out of the car to remove the garbage receptacle that was blocking her car from moving up to the curb, she leaped back into the car, and pressed on the gas pedal. Instead of moving forward, she inadvertently jerked the car into reverse, and gunned it. Thus, the side door was completely ripped from its socket. She was thrown out the driver's side while the automobile slipped down a small embankment. The flying piece of door landed on her leg, creating a deep gash which required multiple surgeries, and grafting. She also broke her pelvis in several places, dislocated her finger, and required extensive hospitalization after surgery.

She was placed in the intensive care unit, after being life-starred by helicopter to an elite trauma-level hospital in the area. I must have called every friend in the entire state of Georgia to pray and intercede for her recovery. She endured multiple surgeries, at least a dozen transfusions, suffered a stroke, a protracted hospital recuperation period, and numerous interventions to heal her aged body. However, the prayers of the faithful were answered. Not only did she survive and completely recuperate, her kidney function, which was only twenty percent before the accident, increased after her multi-trauma. This still astounds her physicians today. The talents and gifts of those who cared for her, the petition of hundreds of prayer warriors, the presence of grace and healing in her life, the love of her family—especially her daughter—who cared for her and remained dedicated to her recovery—were all testimony to the power of God, and His love for her. Obviously, it was not her appointed time to die. Her injury was a witness to family, and the countless men and women who cared for her, that God was sovereign in her situation.

God's Healing through the Extraordinary

When God heals through "extraordinary" means, His intervention causes marvel, curiosity, and further investigation because the occurrence is beyond the usual or established channel of healing.

Divine intervention at this level is meant to profoundly affect an individual in body, mind, and spirit, and ultimately bring faith-benefit to others.

Not too long ago, there was a young woman televised on the news who was diagnosed with a virulent brain tumor (glioblastoma). This incurable cancer attacks brain matter through a series of metastatic webs that grip and choke the brain until the entire brain is destroyed. The mortality rate for this type cancer is one-hundred percent. After doctors tried every intervention imaginable, and the nurse was at the point of death, physicians attempted one final intervention by injecting a genetically modified polio virus (created by a scientist) directly into her brain to attack the tumor. The results were astounding. The virus struck the tumor at its root, destroying the brain cancer over a series of months. God blessed the scientists' remarkable perseverance, intelligence, fascination with the nature of viruses, study of genetic theoretical principles, and painstaking scientific trials. Even though the treatment was tagged "experimental," it launched a series of events, and the platform of discovery not only for the nurse, who was cured, but for the entire nation.

I believe God's Holy Spirit guided the physicians and scientists, blessed their understanding of cell metabolism with the interaction of viruses and cancer cells. He sanctioned their intellectual ability to perform the experimental testing until the specific breakthrough was ready for divine entrance into the world. God knew the exact moment the nurse would need the specific treatment. At the same time, He divinely graced the scientists, and physician(s) to treat the patient by injecting the virus directly into her brain the precise time she mustered strength to consent to the experimental treatment. When everyone lined up with the circumstantial will of God, the results were extraordinary: the invasive tumor disappeared!

God's healing always appears in due time, even in our final season of death. He also approves the healing experiences we have, *so we can help others who are sick.* I call this the "spiritual domino effect" or spiritual law of multiplication. In the case of the nurse who was extraordinarily healed from the brain tumor, additional patients affected by the same brain tumor also benefited from the initial experiment. Thus, another woman residing in the state of Georgia with the same type tumor was helped by living seventeen months beyond her anticipated time of death. I remember seeing her interviewed on TV. What a godly, brave woman, courageous husband, and beautiful family. They expressed gratitude for the extended time they had with her. Another gentleman, who had prior chemotherapy and radiation for the same type tumor, experienced rapid results after the virus was injected into his brain. He also shared his valiant story in the media. Every person involved served a loving, and divine purpose individually and collectively, which benefited others in some way. The scripture verse from John 4: V 37 witnesses to this timeless reality time and again.

"Thus the saying 'One sows and another reaps' is true."

Healed from her brain tumor, the nurse shared that her experience led her to a desire to work in the field of pediatric oncology with children having similar brain cancers. This is an example of extraordinary healing: many lives affected on multiple levels.

Does this reasoning seem farfetched?

The mind of God is omniscience. In the ethereal realm, the embodiment of non-space, non-time, and the divine state of "I AM" forms perfect awareness in the mind of God. He sees conditions, and cures before they appear in the earthly realm. We do not.

> "Now we see but a poor reflection as in a mirror; then we shall see face to face. Now I know in part; then I shall know fully, even as I am fully known."
>
> (I Corinthians 13: V 12)

The Holy Spirit observes past, present, and future discoveries all at once, approves and blesses their time and purpose for us, even before they manifest on Earth. These orchestrated wonders, and divinely coordinated events occur through the talents of people as evidence of His goodness, and love for us. These events also testify to man's ability to overcome, through the grace of God, challenges and set-backs which ultimately benefit mankind and testify to God's ultimate glory.

God utilizes men and women through miraculous, ordinary, and extraordinary channels as co-creators with Him in the unfolding of His upper story. He is not a gender-biased God. The gifts of the Holy Spirit are given to both male and female, to be used for the edification of the body of Christ. (Acts 3: V 17 – 18)

We are all earthly participants on some level, when it pertains to repairing the body, healing the mind, and influencing the spirit under the permissive will of God. He empowers us to aid, assist others, and offer a measure of healing, and restoration to those who need it. He approves, and blesses our God-given talents, ability to explore, discover, learn, invent, and bless others. The most amazing thing about all of this is, God does not need us to co-create with Him but chooses to do so.

Why?

Because He is a God of community, a God of communication, a God of conscious contact, a God of relational love with Himself and us, and a God who loves endearing connections with His children.

God's Healing Through the Miraculous

God also gives us His power to decree, through the authority of His superior blood, powerful life-giving commands which change dire situations and bring about miraculous results. God orchestrates astonishing events to display His undeniable love, compassion, and power in a direct way through us. This is God's upper story directly manifested in the lower story of our lives through God's people in the Church. Miracles relate to the undeserved, divine favor of God. We cannot work for this favor or strive to make it happen through some magic formula. The word "favor" literally means blessing, grace, promotion, and good fortune.

God's favor through miracles, is a sign that He is with us, and still on the throne.

Miraculous events witness to the wonder, and authenticity of God's irrefutable right hand, despite what science or statistical probability deems near impossible. There is no way the world can explain these events, (despite the vociferous rhetoric of skeptics), except from those who believe in faith, that His divine intervention is possible. Miracles also bring substantiating proof of His presence, awe, a sense of marvel, wonder, and a depth of inexplicable joy to those who experience them.

> "Sing to the LORD a new song, for he has done marvelous things; his right hand and his holy arm have worked salvation for him."
>
> (Psalm 98: V I)

Years before I met my future spouse, he was involved in a serious motorcycle accident. He hit a car head-on and sustained multiple brain and bone injuries. He purchased the whole package: an epidural arterial bleed in the brain, broken, and shattered bones throughout his body, and enough damage from the blow to his head to require urgent brain surgery. He wound up getting an acrylic plate in his head, and had to endure a long, arduous rehabilitation and recovery period. He was confined to a wheelchair for several months, on crutches for a year, and initially suffered from recurrent seizures.

At the time of the accident, "it just so happened" that one of the finest neurosurgeons in the area was on-call at a small-town hospital nearby. As soon as they rushed him by ambulance to the medical facility, they prepped his head for surgery, and dashed him into the operating room. Right from the outset, all the conditions aligned under the protective will of God to spare his life.

But here's the miracle folks, the God-wink, his undeserved favor, blessing, and God's extended right arm, and love of the Father for him. The mortality rate for an epidural (arterial brain) bleed is somewhere around ninety-nine percent. Yet, he is alive and well today. He not only survived the surgery and recuperative period through the faithful prayers of those who loved him, but productively works, and enjoys life with minimal damage and no further seizures from his injury. In short—a miracle on a monumental scale. The incident happened over three decades ago, and yet there have been no further ill-effects since. It's as if the catastrophic accident never happened. This is the favor of God, and I consider it a miracle. . .What do you think?

Small scale miracles also happen. God cares about the little stuff, too!

Not too long ago while I was working, I noticed that the small diamond in the center of my ring went missing. Three silver prongs had broken off the setting, and the diamond had fallen out. I checked the office and women's room at work thinking it had dropped to the floor, but to no avail. I finally called my husband, and shared with him I'd lost the diamond. For some reason, I was calm, and able to release the futility of the event into God's hands.

"Lord, this is only a material thing. If it's lost, it's okay with me. I can always replace it if need be, even though it holds sentimental value in my relationship with my husband. Thank you for showing me the most important things in life have no price tag. My relationship with You is all I need. That, I consider priceless. If it's in Your will for me to find the diamond in this impossible situation, I want to thank You in advance for doing so. Either way, I love You. In Jesus's name. Amen."

I had complete peace.

When I returned home from work early evening I checked the house, floors, and areas where I thought the diamond might have dropped, with no success. Finally, after thirty minutes or so, my husband took me by surprise when he moved in close to me, grinning from ear-to-ear.

"Look what I found!" he stated.

I could not believe my eyes! He was holding my tiny, glimmering rock between his thumb and pointer finger.

"When I was walking into the master closet," my husband shared, "I felt something sharp rub against the sole of my foot. I dug into the fibers of the carpet to see what it was, and sure enough it was your diamond."

Do you believe it? What is the probability that this could happen? I was awe-struck. This was my small miracle, a "wonder moment," and God's endearing way of saying to me;

> *"Here you go Mary. Thanks for affirming your relationship with Me and sharing that it's much more important than your ring. Thought you might like it back."*

God's Healing Through the Supernatural

Finally, when God intervenes supernaturally, a force or event occurs *directly from God* which cannot be scientifically or naturally explained.

As Scripture attests:

> "With man this is impossible, but with God all things are possible."
>
> (Matthew 19: V 26)

Supernatural events show evidence of God's direct, undeniable intervention: Jonah survived in the belly of a whale for three days; Lazarus was raised from the dead; King Nebuchadnezzar attempted to kill Shadrach, Meshach, and Abednego by burning them to death. (Daniel 3: V 16 - 18) He placed all three men in a red-hot blazing furnace to kill them because of their faith. They emerged from the hot oven without even being scorched. Mary conceived Jesus while still a virgin. Jesus changed water into wine at the wedding feast at Cana. Jesus rose from the dead fully alive three days after He was killed.

There are stories of men, women or children who survived devastating events like plane crashes or car accidents when they should have been killed instantly. We read about afterlife experiences from men, and women who are alive after being pronounced dead. We hear about events where the medical community claims one conclusion, and the power of God rips it right out of the water. These stories are not some trick of the mind, cynical or peculiar events meant to entertain us or play a hoax on our imagination. These occurrences defy natural and scientific laws. They lay claim to an extremely powerful, and living God who chooses to act directly according to His divine purpose, whether you choose to believe it or not.

Do I believe supernatural intervention from God is real? Absolutely. *This is the magnificence of God on display to the world!*

Human beings cannot qualify such events, despite how hard they try. Scientists or physicians cannot substantiate them through scientific means because such events defy the laws of nature.

Individuals who experience them are:

1. astounded because these events cannot be explained (they seem too absurd);
2. verbalize amazement when they attempt to share the events; and
3. are profoundly changed by them.

We cannot always fathom these unique moves of God. They are so astonishing; the human mind cannot even process them. The facts just don't add up. We can only stand amazed at the goodness, and greatness of the Lord and accept them in a spirit of faith. These remarkable events occur on God's dime and His dime alone, for His ultimate glory and pleasure.

There are dozens of testimonials both by famous and non-famous people alike, who share how God literally spared them from the grave after they'd been instructed to go home and die due to terminal illness. A popular preacher in the mid-west continues to share the story about his mother who was dying from cancer. The woman, who was gravely ill, gives powerful testimony about her complete healing from the brink of death with terminal metastatic cancer, after being told to go home to die because there was nothing else the physicians could do. She is alive today, years later, with no sign of cancer, completely healed, vibrant, and full of life. She is a living testament to her faith, the power of God at work in her life, and the healing of others through her testimony.

If you are keyed into Christian circles, church communities or attend healing services, you will hear testimonials that include: recovery from partial paralysis after being confined to a wheel chair; healing from disseminated collagen disease; disappearance of brain tumors in children; healing from deadly forms of cancer without use of chemo-therapy; straightening of partially crooked limbs; lengthening of limbs and other supernatural recoveries from cases deemed completely impossible or hopeless. This is the astounding work of our Creator!

In keeping with the fourth spiritual principle:

1. *God's plans for me are always good, in every way. His plans will also set me up for a bright future if I trust Him.*

   "For I know the plans I have for you," declares the Lord,"
   plans to prosper you and not to harm you, plans to give
   you hope and a future."

   (Jeremiah 29: V 11)

2. *I will overcome evil and conquer sin because of the sacrifice on the cross that seals my victory against evil in Jesus.*

   "For though we live in the world, we do not rage war as the
   world does. The weapons we fight with are not the weapons
   of the world. On the contrary, they have divine power to
   demolish strongholds."

   (2 Corinthians 10: V 3 - 4)

3. *I will experience the power of His resurrection in every facet of my life.*

   "In him we have redemption through his blood, the
   forgiveness of sins, in accordance with the riches of
   God's grace that he lavished on us with all wisdom and
   understanding."

   (Ephesians 1: V 7 - 8)

4. *I am empowered through grace to be a good steward of my body through self-care practices which bring glory to God and affirm His work in me.*

"My grace is sufficient for you, for my power is made perfect in weakness."

(2 Corinthians 12: V 9)

5. *When Christ is in me, I can experience His physical and spiritual restoration.*

"And the God of all grace, who called you to his eternal glory in Christ, after you have suffered a little while, will himself restore you and make you strong, firm and steadfast."

(1 Peter 5: V 10)

Again, the words in the Gospel of Mark, ring true,

"Everything is possible for him who believes."

(Mark 9: V 23)

Let Us Pray

Dear Father,

I affirm and acknowledge the power of Your healing through Jesus, and His sacrifice on the cross and resurrection from death. Thank You for revealing Your word to me. My relationship with You places me in a posture as rightful heir to the full manifestation of salvation, and Your healing promise. I receive this salvation, Your protection and healing, deliverance, grace, and the ultimate authority to overcome sin, because of Your superior blood covering, and sacrifice. I believe this to be true, not because of anything I could ever do to deserve it, but because of Your son Jesus, and His love for me.

I thank you for placing me under the pinions of Your wings. By Your stripes I am healed, made whole, and redeemed from the curse. I trust Your plan of healing, restoration, and renewal through or from my illness, and the plan and channel to accomplish it. May it be done according to Your will through the supernatural, miraculous, extraordinary, or the ordinary circumstances in my life.

I believe in faith that Your absolute power will deliver me. Thank you for opening my eyes to the work of Your hands. I love You.

In Jesus's name. Amen.

CHAPTER FIVE

My Story of Healing

When I started my journey of healing from cancer, the disease was well established in my body at least two years before warning signs and symptoms appeared, and I was officially diagnosed.

Following the diagnosis in 2010, I spent five years (while I was metastasized) attempting a holistic approach that included organic foods, detoxing, periods of destressing, exercise, weight loss, filtered water, special vitamins and other wellness treatments—all without success.

The disease of cancer was rooted in my family bloodlines along with other generational health issues. It was a treacherous path relatives and siblings had traveled before me. I found myself walking the same dangerous road.

There were multiple cancers generationally present in my family tree which ran the gamut from breast, brain, stomach, lung, blood, skin cancer (both basal cell and melanoma), liver, and bone. I realized the chance of developing cancer seemed inevitable.

Throughout most of my young adult life I was in overdrive and seemingly bullet-proof; holding dreams and aspirations close to my heart with an over-the-top, passionate "Type-A" personality that pushed me to conquer the world in one fell swoop. These were what I tag my "BC" (before Christ) days!

My diet consisted of fast foods, diet soda, and junk foods high in sugar from which I likely experienced periods of "overdrive" that held me prisoner the better part of my youth. Days were marked by endless activities with friends and family, and infrequent rest periods. I often found myself feeling tired, with little reserve after tending to family, work, and later, with ministry activities. I believe this placed undue strain on my body's defense system, and set me up for the big "C."

I also watched other members of my family (my siblings) develop the dreaded disease. As each matured, health matters changed. The horrendous disease reared its ugly head in most of them, except two siblings. Sarcoma of the bone appeared in one, along with basal cell and melanoma skin cancer; cancer of the colon and subsequent death of another; thyroid cancer with metastases along with melanoma of the skin with yet another; and rare malignant stomach tumors treatable only through surgery with another. Then it was my turn. An onslaught of slow-growing cancerous tumors showed up inside the third portion of my duodenum, with one attaching to the outside intestinal wall adjacent to it, one near my ascending aorta, another near the inner groin, and tiny spreads making their way toward the retro-peritoneal area behind my kidneys. They were fearless and seemingly immortal.

The tumors which invaded my body, although slow-moving, were confident, brazen, and intelligent enough to wreak havoc methodically throughout my entire system. My specific type carcinoma was triggered by an "activated" translocation that occurred within the genetic make-up between two of my genes. One specific gene stepped outside its divinely created role, and quietly switched places on my DNA strand with another, resulting in a mismatch on my genetic filament. Thus, my killer T-cells (which were healthy), did not recognize the tumors as foreign. The cellular renegades had changed their protein sequence on the surface of my white blood cells, tricking my destroyer T-cells into believing the cancerous cells were, in fact, normal.

I often wondered if taking hits along the way with colds, exposure to sickness or ignoring my health in prior years had lowered the threshold in my body, allowing for the metabolic and genetic change which triggered the menacing disease. As I've already said, I wasn't always a successful steward of my health in earlier years, even though appearance-wise, I looked healthy. Whatever led to this pivotal point in time, I was diagnosed with cancer, my type being coined as "incurable." I was frightened, and emotionally shocked that God would *allow* this.

In addition, my first encounter with the disease happened during a time when the international ministry I'd launched was growing by leaps and bounds. Multiple countries and international partners were coming on board, volunteer participants were increasing, and donations were on the rise. The vision was scripturally solid, and the work was thrilling; we were the hands and feet of Jesus in poverty-stricken, remote areas of the world for those who had little medicine, compassionate care or the experience of God's love through His word. My heart was full. Our workers were all volunteers yet privileged to bring compassionate care to isolated people groups in secluded areas of the developing world. It was an honor to serve, and show the restorative power of Jesus with men, women, and children who rarely heard about or experienced the impact of the Gospel of healing.

As founder and president, I carried what I now recognize was an exaggerated sense of responsibility for the ministry, in addition to holding down a full-time job. It was God's bad timing, so I thought. I could not understand why Christ would give me a vision, then take me out of the picture. I scrambled to put a succession plan in place, lay out funeral plans, write letters to those near and dear to me, wrap up details necessary to close the final chapter of my life, and line up the global outreach pastor of my local Church to perform the memorial service.

I prayed for miraculous intervention and healing. My prayers were seemingly unanswered. I prayed for a supernatural miracle. God was silent. I was anointed by the elders of the Church, (once a month for a period of seven months—a message that I received in a dream-with how I was to petition their prayers) who patiently endured visits from me with love and perseverance. I managed to tease them a bit during appointments about my frequent use of anointing oils (which they utilized to pray over me), and how I was depleting Church supplies! I even claimed the disappearance of the tumors, stating in faith that God had healed me. All to no avail. It was one thing to claim a personal conviction of future healing, but quite another to try to manipulate the God of the universe to heal me in the way, and time I thought He should.

As time passed, I associated the defiance of my own cells with the fallen nature of humanity itself. I believe there is a core resistance inside each of us (even down to the cellular level), which attempts to counter the divine workings of God. This resistance, intertwined with our inherent nature to rebel, acts out in real time, creating dis-ease in our bodies.

He divinely constructed my cells to act within my best interest, perform in accordance with the system He divinely created, and protect me until my return home. However, there was a pack of cells defiantly growing inside me doing the exact opposite. Isn't that cellular rebellion related to our fallen nature, and separation from the perfect will of God?

As time moved forward, I realized the diagnosis of cancer was not punishment from God. I was spiritually redeemed by Christ, yet plagued by a living war inside of me between the forces of my flesh nature, pitted against the victory of God's word rooted in my spiritual nature. At times, I felt uncomfortably close to death, even questioning whether my beliefs were real.

Would I be spared to complete my work? Would physical healing win the day? Would victory be mine?

My prayers were answered, but not in the way I thought. There were spiritual lessons to be learned along the way.

> "Wait for the Lord; be strong and take heart and wait for the Lord."
>
> (Psalm 27: V 14)

At times, waiting on the Lord is a necessary part of healing. My timing was not the same as God's. Even though waiting on Him seemed grueling, it was not wasted time. In fact, during my "delayed" healing period, He not only carried me every step of the way, He taught and trained me through the storm. I learned valuable spiritual lessons that solidified my relationship with Him and others, while He prepared, and fashioned my future destiny.

Everything in our lives, even illness, has an incredible ability to shift us from chaos into order, raise us from despair to peace, catapult us from darkness to light, push us from discouragement to new vision, thrust us from death's door to new life, and propel us from the brink of death to new destiny. In God's kingdom, chaos, and mess re-emerge as treasures of transformation, inner healing, rebirth, and ultimate fulfillment.

God's hand was with me during the times I felt discouraged, while I fought with every ounce of spiritual and physical reserve inside me to beat the disease. I was tempted to believe that God had sent the illness as a test of faith rather than trust He was taking me through the disease to rebuild my faith, and relationship with Him.

There were times I felt cheated, overcome by self-pity, believing life had dealt me a hard blow. I indulged in thoughts about how it was all "so unfair." I was not ready to die. Future years with my husband, family, friends, and ministry would be snuffed out, and my "finishing of the race" squashed under the weight of an incurable illness. It was during those vulnerable and weak moments God was present in powerful and tender ways, more than I could have dreamed possible.

I received inspirational cards out of the blue, phone calls from friends with reassurance, messages of hope through my cell phone, and words of scripture that bolstered my faith.

One night, I received a prophetic word during a healing service at a local church in Savannah, Georgia.

The minister who prophesied over me was a visitor to the Church from out-of-town who did not know my situation. In addition, when Church members stepped up to the line during the altar call at the end of the service, the pastor moved from right to left across the front of the platform. I was at the far-right end of the line. However, he oddly skipped over me, and proceeded to prophesy over every man, woman, and adolescent throughout the remainder of the line. When he reached the end of the row, he returned to me. He was silent for what seemed an eternity then touched my head gently. My eyes were closed, and head tucked downward. I suddenly felt the warmth of his hand.

He whispered softly,

"My child, I have heard your prayers and given you what you have asked. Have I not been near? O daughter of Israel, I have always loved you with an everlasting love; you will spend an eternity with me in heaven."

"You will live long years," the minister additionally prophesied toward the very end of the service. Then again, he repeated, *"You will live long years."*

I cried buckets of tears, deeply touched that the God of the universe would communicate a message to me of that nature. A sensation of intense heat blanketed me from the top of my head to the tip of my toes. I left the service hanging on every word the minister had imparted.

During the weeks that followed, I felt uneasy and perplexed. Why would God, my Father, address me as "daughter of Israel?" I had never traveled to Israel during my ministry activities, even though our ministry financially supported a Christian outreach in another region of the Middle

East. I rummaged through stories of the Old and New Testament weeks after the service, determined to discover the answer.

I learned that throughout history, God changed the names of those He called. Jacob was renamed Israel. Abram became Abraham, the father of all nations. Sarai was called Sarah, the mother of all nations. Saul was renamed Paul, a name testifying to his conversion from a slaughterer to a man of God who promoted the gospel until his death. Simon was called Peter, the rock, commissioned to build Christ's Church.

I was renamed "Daughter of Israel," meaning one who wrestled with God, but prevailed. Seven years had passed while I carried the disease of cancer inside me before I received the prophecy. Over the past five of those years, I fervently believed, and hoped that God would deliver me through a supernatural or miraculous healing. However, He did not.

Yet, I did receive healing and my tumors did disappear, just as He promised.

As we read in the Psalms,

> "Because he loves me," says the Lord, "I will rescue him; I will protect him, for he acknowledges my name. He will call upon me, and I will answer him; I will be with him in trouble, I will deliver him and honor him. With long life will I satisfy him and show him my salvation."
>
> (Psalm 91: V 14 - 16)

God's love and faithfulness prepared my soul long before the prophecy occurred. There were spiritual signs and messages along the way, symbolic dreams of love and encouragement appearing on and off years before I received treatment. I treasured each of them, holding them close to my heart like a mother hen tending to her baby chicks. I carefully tucked them away in my journal, and committed them to writing, reading them during the times I needed them most.

In retrospect, the Lord created priceless memories with me over many years, all in preparation for the blow I would receive. These messages would bring solace, and comfort to me during my trial.

Throughout the six-month period I received the poisonous treatments, God lovingly and tenderly renovated and reconstructed my life as daughter, young girl, woman, wife, professional leader, and child of God. I had a fiercely independent spirit. While the intensity and passion inside me served the workload in the ministry, it also imposed unrealistic demands on myself, and others who genuinely loved me. There was little option but to slow down and lean on family and friends to make it through. This was especially true during times when chemotherapy took its toll leaving me weak, breathless, and unable to walk. Jesus was reconstructing me from the inside out and the outside in, and I didn't like it.

On one occasion, when I felt exceptionally discouraged, I saw a message on my phone through social media sent by a mega-Church in South Carolina. I felt God directly speaking to my heart when I read it. It summed up my situation perfectly:

"The storm that God sent you into was not meant to destroy you, but to strip some things away so He could rebuild your faith on the solid rock of Christ."

The Fifth Principle

Absence of direct action by God through supernatural or miraculous means is not an indication that you've been abandoned or will not be healed.

There are many diseases besides cancer from which men, women and children suffer, which are equally devastating. My journey was by no means unique or indicated that God did not love me, was abandoning or rejecting me. Quite the contrary. Scripture states:

> "So do not throw away your confidence; it will be richly
> rewarded. You need to persevere so that when you have done
> the will of God, you will receive what he has promised."
> (Hebrews 10: V 35 - 36)

The fifth principle supports scriptural wisdom and truth. God can do infinitely more than we could ever ask or dream of, but, here's the catch—*in His way and timing*. Remember, His ways are not our ways. His method and approach for healing is higher than ours. Our judgement and reasoning are extremely limited. Most times, we *think* we've relinquished control, and placed our situation in the hands of God, when in fact, we are still holding tightly to the reigns. On other occasions, we may want to give up. We mistakenly believe that if God hasn't intervened on our behalf instantaneously, supernaturally or through a miracle, our prayers for healing have been stamped, "Denied." This could not be farther from the truth and is, in fact, a lie.

Many evangelists who have large followings, endorse supernatural and miraculous healing as the only paths in which God works or moves. While it is emphatically true that God heals through these channels, the infallible love of God for us is served and manifested through multiple avenues. At times, He chooses to heal not only through the supernatural, and the miraculous, but through ordinary and extraordinary paths (His permissive will) as discussed in earlier chapters. We see evidence of this, especially in the Old Testament.

If we remain steadfast, confident, and rooted firmly in faith, His promise of healing will not only be ours for the taking, it will manifest in its due time, season and reason. Materialization of the channel and type healing God designates for us, is important, and serves a divine purpose in God's perfect plan for us.

However, the evil one will prey on you. He will try to convince you that God has abandoned you. He'll attempt to destroy credibility of God's relationship with you by introducing doubt, despite the marvelous ways God is intervening on your behalf. Remain faithful. When the *"The Victory Dance of God"* is moving in perfect harmony with your life, His orchestrated steps will not only accomplish His perfect plans, purposes and healing, but His moves cannot be beat!

Just as the channel of healing He chose for my life was unique to me, His choice of healing for your life will be unique for you.

My spiritual growth and personal relationship with Jesus catapulted during the endless days I received chemotherapy, endured after-effects from low blood counts, bruising from low platelet counts, and even swollen limbs from large doses of prednisone. My husband called my feet the Pillsbury Doughboy feet! I experienced labored breathing, loss of appetite, physical bone pain, kidney, and respiratory infections from low white blood cell counts, weakness, weight loss, and severe fatigue. I was a mess. God lovingly knew it, and I knew it.

I leaned long and hard on His shoulder during difficult days, while His rock-solid presence, and endless comfort carried me through the aftermath after each treatment was complete.

As time moved forward, my inner spirit shifted from survival mode to a mindset of confidence and peace. I internally refocused my spiritual outlook from a warring mentality to a spirit of surrender; from periods of doubt to faith-filled moments of acceptance. God's inner healing flowed through me like a gentle breeze. Insights emerged from the Holy Spirit which spoke to me about areas in my life which needed healing.

One area to be addressed was my tendency to be a "driver" who pushed myself, and others to keep up with demands. I needed to have my hands in everything. My faith, at times, was weak. Instead, I liked my own will, and way about things, and was a master at dictating—to God and others how I thought He wanted me to work, act, and move on His behalf with the ministry. I confronted my pride, ego, and the erroneous notion I was the only person who could run the operational piece of the ministry that I founded.

After treatments, I was exhausted, resentful, and disillusioned with operational workloads with the nonprofit, and wanted to quit, especially after trudging through secular duties at my day job. Discouragement ripped through my heart with seemingly no way out except to confront the pain. It was during this heavy-duty renovation, and inner major repair work, God was, unbeknownst to me, rebuilding my heart and spirit from the ground up. He entered the chaos and mess for a reason.

It was time, and I was ready.

He revealed that I had an exaggerated sense of self-importance which compensated for feelings of insecurity.

Even though my passion and heart to serve Him was authentic on one level, He showed me that my need for control was intermingled with the pain of rejection experienced in childhood, adolescence, and early adult years.

In childhood years, and early adolescence, I was a "mis-fit" like many children my age. In late adolescent, to mid-adult years I faced unequal treatment as a woman, about which I remained silent. There were times I was viewed as stupid or "blond," and was discounted for promotions, despite my intelligence or genuine efforts to support and help. I shouldered put-downs because of my gender, and at times was blocked from participating in activities due to gender bias, jealousy or cruelty on the part of others. For reasons unknown to me, I was never placed in work situations which matched my extensive education, experience or training. There were times I was underpaid for the value, and worth I would bring to a job. Through the heart-wrenching revelation of this reality, God whispered a fundamental truth to me about my personal relationship with Him:

"My child, you need never seek validation from the world. My love and acceptance of you is endless and unchanging. It is more than enough."

It's one thing to understand this truth on a cognitive level, yet quite another to experience it on a heart level.

However, suddenly, things changed. The need to prove my worth as a woman was no longer present. The desire to people-please or muster endless energy in relationships that were not based on mutual respect or concern was no longer important. I finally realized on a heart level that my self-esteem, and dignity were rooted in God's love, and not contingent on my education, multiple degrees or what others thought of me.

God simply loved me, wholly and completely.

For the first time in my spiritual journey, the light bulb switched on. I experienced new confidence and vitality, a release from the grip of other people's opinions, a renewed, and deeper call in my relationship with Jesus, and others. I felt a repaired sense of purpose in my journey and calling. I confronted and accepted my limitations, and understood on a heart level, God's validation of me regarding my self-worth. This brought new spiritual confidence, and a rejuvenated sense of spiritual tenacity rooted in His power. I was finally able to surrender the hurt, frustrations, and seemingly insurmountable challenges, and obstacles associated with cancer, the ministry, and past relationships. I also realized that it was okay that I could not run it all, do it all or fix it all. He showed me,

"With Me in you, you are more than enough."

I was finally released from the pressure of performing to the expectations of others and felt genuinely accepted by Him as a woman of God, faults and all.

This personal wake-up call forced me off my personal throne to rethink priorities, go easy on myself and others, spend more time with family, forgive myself often, take time to process, enjoy other activities, and not be so driven in my chosen work. It also helped me to rearrange business matters, take rest breaks, occasionally say "no" to friends and not feel guilty. I was able to schedule needed time to rejuvenate, savor downtime, and finally, talk with God about completion of my destiny through His eyes, and not my own. I started asking other ministry partners and participants to take over more of the ministry's decision-making. It was time for other members to greater utilize their gifts and talents to benefit God's work in the ministry. They did so with a true spirit of excellence.

God was also honing and preparing me to write my first book, a task put on the back burner for years because of the distractions in my life, and whirlwind of activities around me which left little time for writing. I loved to both write and speak. I realized God was sharpening my skills through daily teaching assignments in my secular job in preparation for future speaking engagements.

As my organization's undertakings, and regular job duties balanced out, the cloud lifted, and tides turned in my favor.

Our lives take on profound meaning when we're ready to accept the truth about ourselves, seek forgiveness, and move forward. This is the essence of healing from the "inside out." When we're broken enough, fragile enough, and sick enough, when denial is stripped away by suffering, when truth is raw, and lies bare on the heart and soul, God swoops in with His marvelous hand, and rebuilds us from the inside out.

Remarkably, through God's grace, I continued working through the entire experience, except on days when I received treatment. His abundant grace poured into my life through ambassadors of love. My husband, family, and friends stepped up to assume chores at home while colleagues at work stepped in, quietly picking up the slack on "bad days." He sent Christian brothers and sisters from our Church community to help overcome periods of pessimism, while I learned vital spiritual lessons about my life. He comforted me through prophetic dreams, messages from scripture, favorite songs, and consoling words precisely when I needed them. During the six months I endured harsh chemotherapy treatments, I simultaneously received six months of Godly fortitude and blessing.

God sent cooks, cleaners and emotional supporters. He placed me in the hands of caring physicians, nurses, and physician's assistants. He provided for our household financially. There were exorbitant expenses from the chemotherapy drugs. My insurance covered every dime. I felt genuinely blessed as I watched Him protect my family, and shelter me beneath the pinions of His wings.

On December 29th, 2015, seven months from when the first treatment was initiated and approximately seven years from when the cancer first started, I was officially declared metabolically cancer free. My PET and CAT scans came back showing the cancer had vanished. I was in remission. Renegades gone. Tumors obliterated. Inner failures and defects reconciled. My inner home survived God's deep cleaning and scouring. The prayers of the faithful were honored, and the oil of gladness was upon my head. I was filled with tears of joy. God extended my life, so I could complete my destiny just as He'd promised. Jesus and I shook hands. I accepted the new blueprint for my life, and with heartfelt gratitude, thanked, and praised Him for the reconstruction and renovation He performed from the inside out, and the outside in.

> "In God, whose word I praise, in the Lord, whose word I praise—In God I trust; I will not be afraid. What can man do to me? I am under vows to you, O God; I will present my thank offerings to you. For you have delivered me from death and my feet from stumbling, that I may walk before God in the light of life."
>
> (Psalm 56 V: 10 - 13)

The Seven Gifts

There are seven gifts an individual receives when God chooses to heal through extraordinary or ordinary means as He did with me. These gifts bolster the soul and spirit during times of crisis. They provide periods of perseverance and strengthen character. They increase faith. They bring spiritual revelation for the good of the soul and supply ample amounts of reserve while God is physical restoring, renewing, and strengthening us behind the scenes. The gifts also bring a spirit of steadfastness while waiting for physical transformation to emerge from the chaos. If God is taking you this route, be prepared: stand firm in faith; He is course-correcting your life for some greater purpose.

The first gift: *Perseverance*

"I will persevere."

Perseverance is a form of tenacity. It cultivates inward spiritual determination and strength regardless of the circumstances surrounding your illness, or the sense of being overwhelmed by your situation. Spiritual tenacity requires a time of waiting while you remain encouraged until your healing manifests in the flesh. When fully operational, this virtue produces Godly purpose, and a sincere desire to hang on despite your situation. Your endurance will be rewarded. The Holy Spirit delivers streams of consolations interspersed with periods of physical and mental relief to support and comfort you during your period of trial.

In 2 Thessalonians 2: V 15 - 17, we learn the value of tirelessly holding fast to scriptural principles as a matter of will and not emotion, despite feelings of weariness. When we endure *through* our circumstance, we are essentially relying upon, and leaning on God to deliver us from the mental, emotional, physical, or spiritual burden without complaint. Psalm 27: V 14 also speaks about this matter. We are to wait patiently on the Lord. During periods of waiting, and steadfastness never doubt that God is working behind the scenes.

The second gift: *Persistent Prayer*

"I will pray every day."

Persistent Prayer is a vital component in your relationship with God. Pray unceasingly. Bring your sincere communication and petitions before the throne of God, and place scriptural claim on His promises to heal you.

In Philippians 4: V 6 – 7, we are told;

> "Do not be anxious about anything, but in everything, by prayer and petition, with thanksgiving, present your requests to God. And the peace of God, which transcends all understanding, will guard your hearts and your minds in Christ Jesus."

Scripture instructs us about how to approach God in prayer:

First: Offer sincere praise, exhortation and thanksgiving for all that God has done for you.

Second: Spend quiet time in reflection and evaluation, asking Jesus to forgive you for any sin you have committed in thought, word or deed which has separated you from Him.

Third: Ask the Holy Spirit to intercede before the throne for your healing. This is confirmed in Romans 8: V 26 - 27, which describes how the Spirit helps us in our weakness. Also, James 5: V 16 shares with us that our prayers are not only pleasing to God, they can change our circumstances, and cause a reaping of favor on us. Finally, thank God in advance for the outcome He's already performed on your behalf within His will for your life, believing it is complete in the spiritual realm.

The third gift: *Courage*

"I will embrace courage."

Courage is the opposite of fear. Scripture shares with us,

> "You will not fear the terror of night, nor the arrow that flies by day . . ."
>
> (Psalm 91: V 5)

Cast down every stronghold or vain imagining that exalts itself against the power of God, and stand firmly on His word, despite signs that seem contrary to the manifestation of your healing. Courage is proactive, meaning, it affirms total trust in God's plan and purpose despite what you see in the natural. It additionally asserts trust in Christ, and His power to deliver you in whichever path He chooses.

The fourth gift: *Self-Control*

"I will practice self-control."

Self-control neutralizes the tendency of the flesh to make hasty decisions which counter the leading of the Holy Spirit. Control versus self-control are as far from each other as east is from the west. Without spiritual self-control guided by the Holy Spirit, you can delay your healing, harm your progress, or force outcomes to manifest outside the permissive will of God in your situation. When we practice spiritual self-control, we gain invaluable wisdom to act in accordance with the promptings of the Holy Spirit.

The fifth gift: *Spiritual Guidance*

"I will seek spiritual guidance."

Spiritual guidance is vital, provided it comes from reliable, trusted, and spiritually sound individuals. Ask your heavenly Father to bring into your path individuals who can offer Godly advice, and scriptural grounding during your journey. This can be a person who is firm in their faith, established, and seasoned in the Church community, knowledgeable and informed about biblical principles, and a long-time confirmed member of a Church congregation.

There will also be periods the Holy Spirit will guide or speak to you directly. If this is the case, here are some biblical principles Isaiah 30: V 21 shares with us:

> "Whether you turn to the right or to the left, your ears
> will hear a voice behind you, saying, 'This is the way; walk
> in it.'"

It is important to test the spirit to ensure that the voice you're hearing conforms with scripture. There are three internal voices which compete for our attention:

Ego: This is self-centered me-talk. It is cerebral in nature that speaks to us through our internal feedback system generated by the impulses of the flesh. It arises from the natural mind.

The Holy Spirit: This is the voice of God which emanates through a loving, and powerful spirit of love, which brings encouragement and guidance. He speaks to us through the spiritual mind of man conveying to us, heart-felt knowledge, and truth in conformity with biblical fact. This voice always bears fruit in our lives consistent with the nature of God, confirmed through scripture.

Satan: This is the voice of evil. It speaks to us with half-truths, and tones of condemnation. It entices us to defy God through deception, temptations or other forms of sin. It triggers feelings of confusion or doubt. It badgers us with unholy, unrighteous thoughts aimed at directing us away from God. This voice arises in us through our flesh or fallen nature.

If the internal voice you are hearing is directing you to act contrary to the nature or spirit of God (for example, urging you to harm, kill yourself or another), or tempting you to sin in any way, this is *not* the voice of God or Holy Spirit. It is your own voice, will, or voice of the meddler (evil one). Quickly use the commands you learned earlier in my book:

"In the name of Jesus of Nazareth and the power of His superior blood sacrifice, I command you into silence. Depart from me. You have already lost the battle. Victory is Christ's. He will guide me and give me His eternal voice, and wisdom in this situation."

I guarantee you, if the voice is perpetrated from satan, he will flee immediately.

The sixth gift: *The Word of God*

"I will read Holy Scripture every day. It is actual medicine for my thought-life and physical body."

God's word is power-packed with medicine for the body, mind, and soul. It's advisory in nature, consoling, victorious against sin, wise in counsel, foolproof, loaded with wisdom, practical for every age, triumphant against satan, and according to Proverbs 3: V 8, delivers health to your body, and can even bring actual nourishment to your bones.

The Psalms uplift our spirit. Proverbs instruct us. The Book of Job brings us hope through stories associated with life's challenges, loss, or defeat. The Book of John instructs us. The accounts of Matthew, Mark, and Luke affirm the retelling of God's story; and His death and resurrection power in our lives.

Finally, the gift which supersedes the six gifts listed before it, that impels God's hand to act and move on your behalf is:

The seventh essential gift of: *Faith*

"I believe that God is real, and His promises of healing are absolutely true. They will be manifested exactly the way His perfect plans, and purposes for my life will glorify Him, and benefit my heart, body, mind, and spirit."

Belief is a powerful tool which places claim on God's healing promises. Jesus specifically asks you to trust Him with your whole heart and soul. Put aside the limited understanding you have about your situation. Your task is to remain steadfast, and confident knowing that everything that is happening to you is working for your good. The unfolding of His promise, the certainty of His word acting perfectly on your behalf, and all the divine interventions unfolding in and around you, (whether you are aware of them or not), is *The Victory Dance of God* over you. You can therefore claim, whatever the outcome, "His Promise of Healing is complete!"

Let Us Pray

Dear Father,

I praise You and adore You. I acknowledge You as the great God of the universe. You are the Divine Physician, the Alpha and the Omega, the Beginning and the End. You are magnificent, infinitely holy, perfect, loving, creative, merciful, and all-knowing. You are worthy to be praised!

You created the Heavens and the Earth. You called me forth to know, love, and serve you. I am forever grateful to you O God. You are the true resurrected Jesus, the powerful, and mighty Lord, my spiritual truth, and provider of all wisdom and knowledge for eternity through Your Holy and beloved Spirit. You are the rose of Sharon, the King of Jerusalem, the great I AM, the great encourager. You are the only one true God. From age to age You call a people to Yourself. Thank you for calling me, and for choosing me as Your very own.

I now thank You for my healing. I acknowledge Your loving grace, Your mercy, and the power of Your resurrection in my body, mind, and spirit.

Thank you for restoring, renewing, and rejuvenating me O God, so that I may serve Your purposes throughout my life, and testify to Your power and glory. I await in faith and excitement for the full manifestation of my healing. I believe in Your power to restore me through the channel of healing prepared just for me.

It is in the name of Jesus, your son, I pray and truly say, Amen.

CHAPTER SIX

Evil, Sin and the Powers of Darkness: Herein We Suffer

Things are not as they seem. We live in a dual reality: one we see, one that is hidden. Evil is inevitable, and so is its influence from the underworld.

The spiritual world, which consists of angelic beings and satanic forces (or fallen angels), are invisible to the naked eye. Though they remain hidden by the "veil," and for the most part cannot be visualized, both exist with the ability to influence humanity, and our planet.

In this chapter, we will talk about the uncomfortable subject of evil. We will bring it into the light, expose it, and see it for what it is. We will then move forward, take what we have learned into the future; recognize it, deal with it, and use the spiritual tools we've been given to defeat it.

Evil will always be stronger than the ability for us to resist it *on our own power*. We will never be able to meet evil head-on through our limited flesh nature. We can only defeat it through Christ. The force of Christ in us will always be greater than the power of evil around us, equipping us with the capacity to defeat evil attacks or direct assaults from the devil. Thus, we need to be ready to counter evil or its influence by putting on the full armor of Christ to wage spiritual warfare. The reason why God's word teaches us to dress ourselves in the complete protective covering of Christ is clear: when one area of our life is exposed to it, all areas become vulnerable to strikes from the enemy. Maintaining protection through Christ's blood covering daily in body, mind, and spirit is essential. Here is a list of the symbolic armor we must put on according to Ephesians 6: V 14 - 17:

1. the Helmet (the word of God to protect your mind);
2. the Belt (His truth, girded around you, which helps keep everything you think—spiritually in perspective, and every action you take—under Godly order);
3. the Breastplate (the spirit of righteousness which conforms you to a Godly way of life);
4. the Shield (the ability to fend off attacks of the enemy through Christ's blood covenant);
5. the Sword (the word of God which cuts to the marrow, and heart of the matter); and
6. the boots (your feet, fitted with readiness to walk in the ordained path God has for you).

As I discuss the powers of evil in this chapter, I pray in agreement with Holy Scripture, and the promises of God through His son Jesus; that you will not entertain the spirit of fear as you read this chapter, but remain in a spirit of peace, of sound mind and heart, and rooted in the word of God as your mental armor.

Let us pray.
In the name of the Father, Son and Holy Spirit;
"I surround you with the light and love of Jesus. I encamp Christ's covenant of protection around you. I place Christ's shield over you to defend you, and His armor to safeguard you from any darts of the enemy in body, mind, or spirit. I bind and sever all fear in the name of Jesus. I claim Christ's sheltering around you, and place you under the pinions of His wings. I declare, that no evil will touch you. You will complete the chapter in a spirit of deep peace, and confidence in the love and power of Christ. In the name of Jesus I pray. Amen."

My prayer is that all Christians remain wise, informed, and knowledgeable through the power of the Holy Spirit, about the capabilities and tactics of the underworld; why evil entities exist, what satan's modus operandi is, and what demons can and cannot do. Please know, and for this I am certain. We are "not" summoned by Scripture, to obsessively focus or place undue attention on satan. However, we are not called to be naïve, either. As children of God, we are expected to become spiritually informed by studying the word of God so that we may recognize evil, sin in ourselves, other people, places, and events. We must also remain ready to courageously activate Christ's blood covenant when immediate spiritual intervention is necessary. This is part of our Godly inheritance. We are given spiritual tools as God's children and must use them.

Here's the good news. It doesn't matter what you've done in the past. Healing is one spiritual step from redemption, after you've accepted Christ into your life. When you make a soul-saving decision to fully embrace Jesus and seek repentance, all is forgiven. The slate is wiped clean. The spirit of Christ becomes God's dwelling place within you. It's the stronger power source, and commanding resistance against the schemes and tactics of the enemy. It's also the spiritual portal to His love, light, and forgiveness in body, mind, and spirit.

We are all vulnerable. No one enters the world free from the propensity to commit wrong doing, serious sin or suffer from its effects. Sin separates us from the light, and divine flow of Christ. When we give into temptation, satan uses it to dismantle us from having a power-filled spiritual relationship with Jesus.

Sin wages resistance to healing. Evil rages war against God.

It all comes with a price, and reaps serious consequence. Unless you carry God's light within you, and root yourself in His word, and the Christian community (a channel which brings fortification, forgiveness, restoration, healing and deliverance), you'll succumb to the opposition, and fall.

Rooting yourself in a strong faith-based community is paramount to spiritual health, growth, and wellbeing. In Ephesians 2: V 19 - 22, scripture shares with us about the secret of remaining individually and collectively strong *as a fortress* during physical, mental or spiritual assault.

> "Consequently, you are no longer foreigners and aliens, but fellow citizens with God's people and members of God's household, built on the foundation of the apostles and prophets, with Christ Jesus himself as the chief cornerstone. In him the whole building is joined together and rises to become a holy temple in the Lord. And in him, you too are

> being built together to become a dwelling in which God
> lives by his Spirit."

We go about living our daily lives, and for the most part remain completely unaware of unseen forces warring behind the scenes. We know evil exists. Scripture tells us. We experience it individually, collectively, and the effects of it in our communities, and in the world around us. However, if you are rooted in Jesus, the prayerful protection of the people of God, through the Church, and remain equipped through the power of God's word, wicked influences or evil activities will have no authority over you, nor trigger a spirit of fear or timidity. Fear is not from God, but spiritual wisdom is. We are apprised by scripture to remain aware, stay informed, and guard our hearts.

The world tells us through a cliché, that ignorance is bliss. I beg to differ. In the spiritual world, *ignorance is not bliss*. Invisible forces exist which continually battle to destroy the validly of God's power in your life, mine, and the lives of those around us.

Remember, satan has absolutely "no" authority over you. His power is rendered useless through the authority Christ gave you in His name. You will need to know how to use this authority though, when situations arise that will require you to render the weight and intensity of evil, powerless.

Your mind is the battleground where struggles between good and evil take place. It is also holy territory where powerful healing and transformation transpires to defeat the power of sin, mental, emotional, spiritual, physical disease, and forces of evil attempting to target your life, and snuff-you-out in body, mind, and spirit.

When evil is in full throttle, it manifests itself as a full assault, lofty defiance, or warring directly against God by satan, or the wicked manifestation of satan through the possession of man. An example of a direct assault through satan, would be the angelic wars that took place prior to the beginning of time when angels were dispelled from heaven because of their defiance against the creator.

When sin is expressed, it is communicated through a willful act by man, either in body, mind, or spirit, that causes a rift or separation in ones relationship with God. In this case, we see an example of this with Adam and Eve, when they were removed from enjoying a perfect bond with God in the garden of Eden due to their willful decision to disobey Him. It reaped consequence for them, and us.

There are numerous titles for the devil in the Old and New Testament. The word satan (Mark I: V 13) is described as someone who tempts. The fallen angel is also referred to as the accuser of our brothers. (Revelation 12: V 10)

Other names include: ". . . a roaring lion looking for someone to devour." (I Peter 5: V 8); ". . .beelzebub, the prince of demons . . ." (Matthew 12: V 24); " . . . the dominion of darkness" (Colossians I: V 13 - 14); " . . .leviathan, the gliding serpent. . ." (Isaiah 27: V I); ". . .angel of the abyss. . ." (Revelation 9: V 11); "Your enemy the devil prowls around like a roaring lion looking for someone to devour." (I Peter 5: V 8); ". . .the tempter. . ." (Matthew 4: V 3); ". . . the powers of this dark world and against the spiritual forces of evil in the heavenly realms. . ." (Ephesians 6: V 12); "The thief. . ." (John 10: V 10); ". . .a star that had fallen from the sky to the earth. . ." (Revelation 9: V I); ". . .the man of lawlessness. . ." (2 Thessalonians 2: V 3 - 4); ". . . a murderer. . .the devil. . . the father of lies." (John 8: V 44)

Although there are numerous names identified with satan, his role, mission and demonic activity remain the same. He is not only against God, he is against all humanity.

Lucifer is a powerful and radiant angel of light removed and "cast down" from the heavens because of pride, covetousness, jealousy, resistance, and arrogance against God and His divine laws.

Scripture clearly articulates satan's breeding ground as planet Earth. He is not only real; he subsists as a fallen spiritual being whose bottom-line strategy is to convince you that God does not exist, strike against you, rob you from your rightful inheritance, and strip you from the rewards of heaven. He is specifically assigned to deprive you of God's light, love and healing, and make your life miserable.

All of us are deeply connected to the physical and tactile world because of our flesh nature. Although we primarily seek healing on a physical level, the secret of healing in the physical realm is directly related to life-giving restoration through the *soul, mind, and heart on a spiritual level, through the power of the Triune God.* You can't have one without the other. The body and spiritual mind are not separate, but deeply intertwined with one another through the way God made us. Satan always seeks to destroy man's heart, mind, and spirit, in addition to man's inclination toward good. Once he does that, he has an "in."

Scripture shares with us that he can also directly attack the physical body.

God created your soul and spirit to be predominantly stronger than your physical flesh or outer casing. Your God-directed spirit will not only unequivocally influence the condition of your flesh, it can influence for the better, even outcomes on our planet. The life force of the Holy Spirit in you is a power-packed spiritual cell that, when fully activated, repairs, changes, transforms, renews, restores, and heals the spiritual and physical reality around you. It also defeats the enemy.

While evil exists to kill and destroy, sin patterns and generational strongholds are used by satan to sever your covenant right to healing, and your relationship with God. Sin is lucifer's GPS system that allows him entrance into your heart and spirit. Once he sets up shop, he is driven, and viciously determined to plant strongholds, wreck your life, cause havoc, incite misery, and snatch you from the healing glory of Christ.

There are three solid tactics discussed later in the chapter which spiritually outsmart satan, capture your life back from the clutches of sin, and enable you to experience pleroma (Greek word for understanding, fulfillment or having the experience of being full of contentment).

The apostle Paul shares a sample of this state of contentment during his trials through the book of Colossians. When you are under the umbrella of spiritual pleroma, the powerful effects of Christ's death and resurrection are in full throttle. It's an insurance package which works for your benefit, informing you that your "house" is covered. You'll know your spiritual policy is working when you encounter deep satisfaction despite mounting difficulties, face intense problems with spiritual resolve, feel protected during unsafe circumstances, undergo severe trials with wisdom and calm, or handle horrific situations with determination and confidence, despite demonic influences attempting to target or rupture your sense of peace or well-being.

You'll know your spiritual policy is deficient when you experience strife, anxiety, fear, panic, feelings of being unsettled, spiritually aloof, or engage in activities that separate you from God. Your spiritual insurance "card" will need major repair if you are experiencing the phenomenon scripture identifies as doublemindedness. This spiritual disease of the soul, from which even pastors and leaders in the global Church can suffer, is more than a "sin issue." It is a form of spiritual instability or wavering in one's inner disposition which causes the acting out of two behaviors (one godly, one ungodly) all in quick succession. It manifests itself as a flipping back and forth, or expression of ungodly deeds alongside Godly activities, which causes confusion and perplexity in the body of Christ.

Examples of doublemindedness include:

1. a pastor, minister or Church leader who maintains an illicit affair (marital infidelity) while charismatically pastoring a Church;
2. a Church that preaches, and teaches the word of God yet knowingly places an individual with a serious sin issue in a leadership position;
3. a believer in Christ who spiritually supports and encourages you but, in the same breath, yells, discourages, abuses, criticizes or belittles you;
4. a minister or spiritual leader who, while preaching the word of God, renders an off-colored joke or ungodly language to appear "hip," or verbalizes a put-down about someone in the congregation in public, after praising them;
5. someone who quotes scripture, but then curses or uses improper language to describe something pertaining to God.

There are at least twenty scriptural verses in the Old and New Testament describing this spiritual stronghold. James I: V 7 - 8 explains this phenomenon as relational instability with God. Other examples of doublemindedness include: praising God with your lips, and in next moment, spewing curse words against a friend or loved one; or agreeing with someone, then verbalizing vicious judgement, or verbal attack against the same person behind their back. These opposing forces which internally war against one another in rapid succession (a house divided against itself), show grave wavering in the core of an individuals' spirit. The behavior often causes bewilderment when others encounter it. It can also occasionally be described, as a "Dr. Jekyll, Mr. Hyde" type personality. Doublemindedness is a spiritual stronghold which obstructs the fullness of the spirit, and requires deliverance.

> "Therefore, since we have been justified through faith, we have peace with God through our Lord Jesus Christ, through whom we have gained access by faith into this grace in which we now stand."
>
> (Romans 5: V 1 - 2)

In other words, we have the power to stand strong against mental, spiritual, or physical storms that rage out of control inside us. Despite circumstances in and around us, we have, through grace, Christ's power, and the tool of godly restraint to help us practice self-control, all while receiving God's full measure of peace.

Imagine having the power to disarm evil spirits or demonic forces, heal relationships, deliver individuals from physical, mental or spiritual illness, and even change the world?

The truth is, we do. We have the authority over evil to spiritually break, smash, strike, cast out, confuse, silence, and send satan and his cohorts back to the pits of hell where they belong. However, it's not the spiritual energy based on your own strength, empty words, voodoo or mumbo-jumbo gibberish rooted in dark-sided spiritualism.

The authority of God's word is a "Holy Declaration." It is backed by the superior sacrifice of Christ's shed blood on the cross as a power source for all God's people. It is the perfect weapon to annihilate the enemy, and command God's victory in situations that are out of control. Jesus's blood covenant not only holds spiritual weight. It is the spiritual substance that moves mountains, engages, defeats, conquers the enemy, and sends satan running in the opposite direction with his tail between his legs!

The Church (or the people of God) are sufficiently armed to avert, and squash evil through Jesus's power, and literally change the world for Christ. Why then, is this not happening? *Why are we not seeing this power fully manifested?* What are the issues?

At times, we neglect to use the authority of His word or call on the superior blood of Christ when we pray over others. Sometimes, we misunderstand how to access or use this covenant authority. Our prayer lives may be insufficient. We have become a culture that is too busy. We are anesthetized, distracted, and overly immersed with processes, regulations, and the demands of life and Christian activities. Our "balance" in life has become bombarded with overstimulation, technical distractions, and social media. We've become uncomfortable verbalizing the authority of Christ in prayer for ourselves or others. Many individuals have stopped going to Church. Authentic relationships are being replaced with the superficiality of wireless phones, and gadgets which talk to us, and follow our commands. We would not be witnessing the rise of evil or the level of powerlessness evident in the world today due to satan, if Christians were effectively utilizing this God-given authority individually and collectively.

I believe a resurgence of Jesus's power in the world (with the people of God) is imminent. Signs, wonders, miracles, and supernatural events are on the horizon. We are in a prophetic season where God is making ready. He is raising up prophets, recharging and equipping the people of God, sharpening our spiritual gifts through the power of His Holy Spirit, and organizing us, through Him, to break the grip of the evil abomination in our age. He is preparing to squash the frenzy of evil infecting God's children, our nation, and our world. He is bringing forth people within the Church, from every nation, who will be obedient, and fully equipped to use *all* the gifts of the Holy Spirit without fear, trepidation or embarrassment. These will be children after God's own heart, the Church within the Church, who will utilize powerful spiritual weapons to fight evil, and change world events through Christ that are leading us down the path of self-destruction and annihilation.

Can you imagine what would come to pass if Christian Churches in every nation of the world decided to unite in prayer and fasting for even thirty days to spiritually disarm the evil strongholds in our country, and those affecting our planet? The vise-like grip of sex slavery would crumble, the spirit of murder would vanish, governmental divisions would evaporate, terrorism would be defeated, dictators would lose their power. Secular men and women of great faith, and character would emerge as ambassadors of truth and righteousness to lead our country.

Where are you, Christ's Church?

You are asleep. Jesus is waiting to manifest His mighty victory through you.

Awake! Rise-up in the powerful name of Jesus! You have covenant authority. Use it.

Lucifer's main objective is to destroy individuals, families, marriage relationships, communities, governments, nations, and leaders in the Church. Legions of evil angels can mobilize under satan's authority. Their assignments, when active, wreak havoc, instigate malicious schemes, and conjure up evil plans to decimate the children of God. They are fueled by other demonic entities with unique assignments that incite risk, wreak chaos, discord, threats and evil dissension.

Demons have the capacity to influence humans, and the environment. However, they do not have the ability to possess or overtake a soul covered under the blood of Jesus unless the individual willingly gives consent.

Satan does not have permission to take your life (as a child of God) prematurely or without God's permission. When an individual has completely rejected Christ, worships false entities or embodies a state of serious sin without repentance, this can open the door to mortal circumstances removing him or her from the divine protection of the Holy Spirit. Consequently, it is possible to die a premature death outside the intended will of God.

As a child of God, the completion of your spiritual mission, and not your age is at the center of God's heart, even though in scripture, we are promised length of days. (Proverbs 3: V 1- 2) In the final analysis, lucifer's period on Earth is limited, even though his defiant spirit refuses to acknowledge that Jesus has already won the victory, and satan's final score card is stamped "defeated."

When a specific sin becomes a pattern with an individual, moves from one generation to the next, or becomes prevalent in communities or countries, it's regarded as an individual, generational, or relational stronghold. Repetitive sin patterns grow, increase in intensity, and can infiltrate into widespread regions. This is satan's mission. Principalities are responsible for creating individual and collective strongholds, regional horrors and atrocities that infect spiritually unprotected areas in the world. (Ephesians 6: V 12)

A principality is a higher level of demon who can influence or take dominion over larger regions or mass populations. Ephesians 2: V 2 describes one such evil ruler as having dominion over the air.

The aim of a principality or prince of demons is to permanently destroy individual(s) by inflicting mass deception or viciously destroying the goodness of God's spirit in the heart of man. (Genesis 3: V 1 - 5)

Through explicit sin strongholds, evil abominations, and other serious atrocities, individuals, large populations or entire countries can be affected. These evil abominations are perpetrated by demonic princedoms who promote evil schemes in populations spiritually unequipped to resist. These groups succumb due to deep-seated atheistic ideologies or reside in weak spiritual communities where there is absence of the word of God or the power of Christ's authority.

Demonic infestations exist in the United States and worldwide, which confirm evil dominions or patterns of wickedness not only exist but have planted strongholds. The capital of Georgia has one of the most prevalent sex-slavery pits in the United States. The Midwest suffers from devastating tornadoes and twisters which decimate and kill thousands. Chicago has become known for intense gun violence and murder. Nevada is plagued by legal prostitution. Suicide is rampant in Tennessee, Missouri, Kansas, and Arkansas. More and more states are legalizing Marijuana in our country, a mind-altering drug which can change the brain chemistry of individuals who use it. There is a serious opioid, heroin epidemic in the United States. Regions of the Middle East are a breeding ground for rape, murder, acts of defilement against humans (particularly women), public punishment killings, and wars in the name of religion. Communism is rampant in East Asia. India is plagued by false deities, worshiping of golden statues, severe hunger, devastating poverty, and vicious cyclones. Africa suffers from bloody civil wars. South and Central America, and the United States, is riddled with cartels, gangs, and drug addiction. The principalities entrenched in these areas cause devastation in their wake. They can only be conquered though the rising light of Mother Church, and the authority of the blood covenant of Jesus Christ.

The Church is the powerful arm of God. Through love, power, the authority of Christ, persistent and unrelenting prayer, fasting, use of all the gifts of the Holy Spirit, and commanding authority of the superior blood of Jesus, the people of God *do have* spiritual power and authority to overthrow, cancel, and squash these demonic influences. The Church must use this authority to reestablish the spirit of Christ in these regions.

While strongholds manifest themselves though repetitive mental, physical or emotional sin pathways, Christians *need to recognize* their signs and effects. We must remain alert and spiritually armed to demolish their influence in our lives, and the lives of others through the sword of the spirit (Word of God). Once a sin pattern or generational grip is broken, it is permanently severed unless the door is reopened to the stronghold through repetition of the same sin.

To experience authentic protection, and healing in body, mind, and spirit, it is important to position oneself in a strong faith-based community of believers (in the Church). I've heard many individuals share with me over the years:

"I don't need Church, it's not for me."

"The Church is full of people who've made mistakes, and have serious flaws." "They are all hypocrites."

"I've been hurt by a member in the Church."

"I am not going back."

"My relationship with God is personal." "I don't need to attend services or worship God in front of others."

"The Church is always looking for money."

"That pastor or minister is imperfect."

"There've been too many wars in the name of religion." "I don't need to be a part of anything associated with the Church."

Truth is, the Church is a spiritual hospital for all of us, as sinners. We have all sinned and fallen short of the glory of God. There is a clear directive through scripture, for man, to be a part of a life-giving community of believers. This group is not comprised of perfect individuals. But it does consist of wonderful men, women, and children who love God, each other, and are trying to get it right. Each of us have a responsibility to maintain a relationship with God by staying connected to the life source He provides for us. His mandate is clear. We are not to travel our spiritual journey alone. The army of God (in the Church community) surrounds, protects, and provides daily prayer support for its members. It's important to have a body of people to pray for you, defend you in battle through prayer, and support you when evil tests or challenges your spiritual capacities. I don't know where I would be today, if I did not have the rock-solid love, and support of my home Church in Savannah, Georgia. I absolutely love the people God has planted in my life, through Christian community.

A senior pastor who shepherded a successful, life-giving, large nondenominational Church in Chicago frequently talked about the power of God, and the Church's influence in the world. His simple yet powerful message? *"The Church is the hope and light of the world."*

When the Church gets it right, it is the conscious, visible sign of God's love, transforming man on the world stage for His honor and glory.

What is the Church's primary role? To share the message of God's love in the world through preaching, and teaching of the Gospel, promote forgiveness of self and others, scripturally challenge the people of God to become better men and women, promote good works, encourage acts of Christian service for the less fortunate, and ultimately defeat principalities in our communities, nation, and world. This is the hope and light of the world about which the pastor speaks. The Church retells the story of God's relationship with man, and bears witness to His powerful authority to transform the world. As an army of God's people, we can do all things through Christ, but nothing through our own power.

There are four powerful tactics the enemy uses to defeat us. These evil schemes are intended to cloud our judgement, distort the truth of God's word, annihilate Jesus's Holy and righteous spirit, crush our soul, and rob us of our rightful inheritance to healing. It's important to recognize the diabolical schemes satan uses to destroy humans.

The four methods satan utilizes are:

1. Persuading: This is demonic swindling of the mind, by coaxing people into believing something is true when it is blatantly false.
2. Convincing: This is proving through a combination of half-truths (human rationality mixed with evil intent, which appeals to one's emotions or through cognitive reasoning), that deceitful principles or humanistic ideologies are godly, when, in fact, are completely opposite to God's word and divine will.
3. Seducing: This is enticement and seduction through one's sexuality or through sensual pleasures, which leads to the acting out of offenses against God through sexually deviant behavior. This can take the form of obsession with pornography, lust, twisted sex, polygamy, sexual orgies, unnatural sexual relations, sado-masochism, rape, sexual domination, prostitution, incest, bestiality, and extramarital affairs.

4. Deceiving: This is the powerful art of evil trickery which wins the minds and hearts of believers, and unbelievers alike. There are different levels of demonic deception which target specific individuals, communities, nations and leaders, followed by mass demonizing of the highest order.

Some or all these tactics used by lucifer, can result in mind control, or be deployed through evil principalities or cohorts which target groups, government entities, and even leaders of nations. A demonic veil covers the eyes, and ears of an individual or population, preventing them from discerning Godly truth. The heart and spirit of man then becomes distorted or deadened. When fully mobilized, these deceptions (perpetrated by a controlling foul principality), compel man to commit wicked acts.

Examples of "severe" demonic strongholds (through physical or mental deception) can include:

*   the killing or extermination of whole populations in the name of . . .;
*   criminals with no moral conscience (psychopaths who maim, cannibalize or kill people or animals for sport);
*   radicalized behaviors of terrorists who are convinced that acts of terror are not only permissible but endorsed by their god. These vicious acts include horrendous forms of killing, sadistic beheading, raping of women and children, limb removal as punishment, burnings at the stake, brutal terrorizing of men, women, and even children; demolishing territories, and dominating regions of land—all in the name of religion.

Evil rulers can easily persuade or deceive groups of individuals into believing that a specific act is not only justifiable but satisfies a higher purpose. Thus, when a demonic spell is cast over a person's mind, a dark, slippery trap ensues—perpetrated by the highest rank of lucifer's armies. Evil clutches the mind and heart of the demonized individual, placing them under a hex. The person becomes spiritually blinded, then enslaved by a form of deceptive wickedness which not only chokes the person's mind, heart, and body, but repeatedly drives the individual to commit horrendous acts of evil. They can even become possessed.

Even though we are witnessing the increase of evil activity in the world today, these type demons have been present per biblical accounts, even before the birth of Christ, and early Church. Their evil ranks are positioned in the higher tiers of the nether-regions of darkness which consist of revolting, fallen angels who lie in wait to destroy the very heart, and spirit of good in man. You will know them by the evil effects they leave in their wake: terror, enslavement, and complete destruction. They are tasked with promoting fear, terror, confusion, lies, and vicious, coldblooded activities (human killings for sport or murderous atrocities) in the name of lucifer. These activities are used to dismantle and destroy God's kingdom. Principalities can only be demolished, and their evil yoke broken through the unrelenting spiritual army of God's people in the Church, through individual and collective prayer, repeated fasting, the power of Jesus's love, and the casting out of these strongholds through the authority of the superior blood of Christ.

Saul (later named Paul by God), was a zealot who believed his mission was to harm, kill, and destroy Christians in the name of religion. He was convinced his actions were not only fueled by obligation but honored religious tradition. He was filled with pride, arrogance, and a spirit of retribution. Further, he was offended by the spirit of Christianity, which he believed threatened religious law. His deluded conclusion: It was his duty to exterminate followers of Jesus.

While his mission seemed certain to him, a powerful demon of the highest order was working behind the scenes to destroy Saul. The areas which opened the door to Saul's demonizing were the sins of:

1. harsh judgement;
2. anger;
3. self-righteousness; and
4. a false conviction about religion.

This pitted him against the power and authenticity of Christ, and was further compounded by powerful trickery introduced to him by a demonic principality. Saul was seduced into believing that Christians were instigators, or false zealots who would take down religious customs rooted in Old Testament tradition. Thus, the devil used Saul's weakness as an open door to cast a diabolical spell of deception over him and halt the destiny God had for his life. It wasn't until Saul had a powerful conversion experience, and his heart was transformed, that he was able to break free of this powerful stronghold, and embrace his new calling.

Acts 9: V 1 - 2 clearly shows that Saul, who was a Roman citizen, was acting out murderous threats and actions against the disciples, and other followers of Christ while attempting to take them as prisoners into Jerusalem. As he neared Damascus, a blinding light threw him off his horse. He fell to the ground when a voice said to him,

> "Saul, Saul, why do you persecute me?"
> "Who are you Lord?" Saul asked.
> "I am Jesus, whom you are persecuting, he replied."
>
> (Acts 9: V 3 – 5)

Though this profound experience, Saul had a life-altering conversion of his soul, and accepted Christ as His Lord and Savior. During the time of this spiritual rebirth, he was repeatedly attacked, physically, and mentally abused, and thrown into prison. Even though he went through a time of great persecution, and experienced the maniacal fury from demonic forces yet again, this time he was granted tremendous grace by the Holy Spirit, given a platform to write, teach, and preach, develop leadership skills, and share the good news of the Gospel through arranged meetings with Jewish leaders before he was martyred for his faith.

Saul did not have a conversion experience through the power of reasoning. His changeover was a *heart-soul alteration* of the highest order in which God's light entered the darkness, chaos, and mess. Jesus penetrated the very core of his soul through an event that completely freed him, changing Saul from the inside out, and the outside in.

Saul was living a deception so diabolically evil he did not even recognize the futility of his own actions. God provided the means to alter the course of his spiritual destiny by allowing Saul to experience physical blindness when he fell off his horse. How metaphorical! He was physically, and internally blinded from God's truth and love. God used the very trial he endured from this blindness, as the vehicle for his transformation, rebirth, and reconnection with the true heart of the Father.

Saul not only had a complete reawakening, he was not the same person anymore. Hence, God renamed him Paul. The sins of barbarity, hatred, pride, prejudice, discrimination, immorality, and acts of murder committed by Saul were washed away by the redeeming love of Jesus. This resulted in a total healing of his heart toward God, which unchained him from the demonic stronghold, and restored his soul to his true destiny, a spiritual life rooted in Christ.

Absence of God in your life, lack of a relationship with Jesus, inadequate spiritual grounding through Gods word, or absence of Godly support will eventually erode God's presence, protection, and obstruct His flow of healing. You will know that satan has gained a foothold, created a stronghold, or set a trap for your life if these danger signs are present:

1. You begin to have continuous feelings of suspiciousness, cynicism, hate or distrust of others, or the Church.
2. You feel arrogant, justified or outraged, harbor a deep grudge against an individual, or isolate from the Church, or group of people associated with the people of God, or become preoccupied with ways to retaliate against individuals who've hurt you or caused you emotional pain.
3. You are turned off by, or disinterested in stories of wholesomeness, goodness or godliness in others, or feel repulsed, angered, bored by, or want to isolate from people you consider "goody two-shoes."
4. You become disinterested with the cause of good, or become obsessed with wanting to pay-back or harm others.
5. You increasingly enjoy watching dark movies or themes connected with evil, or feel attached to movies with demonic themes, feel a connection or attraction to storylines that show murderous violence, rape, gang brutality, or other type stories that are bloody or sinister in nature.
6. You begin to imagine yourself in mental positions of power that involve violence, domination or control over others.
7. You become disturbed when you hear Godly music or discussions about the goodness of God.

8. You set yourself up as the judge, jury or mental executioner of people, places, and things in thought, word or deed.

These mental aberrations, or spiritually bereft behaviors require immediate prayer, intervention, and spiritual deliverance. Satan uses these physical and spiritual strongholds as a foothold to set up camp, enter your heart, and destroy you.

Although we live in the real world, bombarded by sin and violence daily, a heart planted in the soil of the Holy Spirit will not be moved or stirred by evil demonstrations or temptations of this nature. We hold spiritual weapons which not only help us to resist, but remain equipped with the spiritual arsenals to deliver us from evil traps of this nature, or strongholds I discussed earlier in this Chapter.

When you begin a new or renewed relationship with Jesus (before you consciously use your stockpile of spiritual weapons), your ability to resist will be weaker than your inclination to give in. Resistance is a matter of your disposition of heart toward Christ. It is a commitment to your relationship, and a decision to resist sin because you love God. Once the choice is made to choose Godliness, feelings of peace, grace, and strength follow.

To recognize the tactics of the enemy and nature in which satan works:

1. Believe he is real.
2. Recognize his game plan (he is an evil deceiver, persuader, convincer, and seducer).
3. Understand that his main objective is to destroy you.
4. Disavow his power over you in the name and superior blood of Jesus. This opens channels of healing, and spiritual strength to oppose his evil tactics, and plans.
5. Stay away from influences which put you in satan's line of fire.

Scripture gives powerful advice about resisting evil:

"Finally, be strong in the Lord and in his mighty power. Put on the full armor of God so that you can take your stand against the devil's schemes. For our struggle is not against flesh and blood, but against the rulers, against the authorities, against the powers of this dark world and against the spiritual forces of evil in the heavenly realms."

(Ephesians 6: V 10 - 12)

Here are some practical decisions you can make to avoid sin or the risk of an evil encounter:

1. Choose individuals of your same gender with proven character who can support and help you be a better man or woman in the context of Christian community.
2. Find an accountability partner of the same gender (not your spouse), who can tell you the truth about yourself. This would be someone you can trust who will hold you spiritually accountable in your relationship with God, and others.
3. Plant yourself in a faith-based, proven biblical Christian community.
4. Avoid people, and situations which could compromise your commitment to leading a Christ-centered life.

"Therefore put on the full armor of God, so that when the day of evil comes, you may be able to stand your ground . . ."

(Ephesians 6: V 13)

The Sixth Principle

Evil has no power over you. It cannot harm, destroy or overtake you. You are victorious in Christ, armed with the shield of faith, and the power of His word. This enables you to stand firm against the traps and snares of the enemy.

Let's identify some prototypes of evil, sin, and generational strongholds which can prevent us from living a victorious life.

We are all vulnerable to forces competing against God's attention, power, and light. It doesn't matter who you are or what position you hold in life. Whether you are rich, poor, famous, tall, small, large, working, retired, a pastor, minister, teacher, prophet, doctor, nurse, accountant, journalist, secretary, stay-at-home parent, hold a government position or are president of a country. Dark forces continuously work to undermine the creative, holy, and powerful majesty of the supremacy of God manifested through you, His children and all of creation. These evil powers attempt to strike, dethrone, strip the spirit of God in you, and delegitimize the manifestations of His splendor, grandeur, magnificence, and God-given power working through you. Satan often works through individuals who maintain governing responsibilities over large populations to affect the masses. Satan's assignment is to rob, cheat, and steal your spiritual destiny, derail your relationship with God, and permanently remove Jesus out of your life.

In scripture Jesus shares,

> "The thief comes only to steal and kill and destroy; I have come that they may have life, and have it to the full."
>
> (John 10: V 10)

The Mission of God Versus the Sinister Plot of Evil

The light bearing vision and mission of God the Father goes like this:

God's Vision: "I have redeemed you through my son, Jesus. You are free to receive My divine love, joy, power, healing, and peace which I give you through my Holy Spirit. You are rightful heirs to the kingdom of heaven through Me, where I have prepared a place for you."

God's Strategy: "I have equipped you with everything you need through the power of My love and the authority of My word to be victorious in the world."

God's Tactic: "I will give you the sword of the Holy Spirit to defend you in battle, the breastplate of truth to recognize the lies of the enemy, the helmet of salvation to protect your mind from the attacks of the enemy, and the power of My word to stand strong against the powers of darkness."

God's Mission: "I have won the victory over evil. The gates of hell cannot prevail against Me. You can enter eternity with Me. The price for your redemption has been paid in full."

The dark and sinister vision and mission statement of evil goes like this:

Satan's Vision: Evil will destroy the people of God as quickly as possible before Christ returns.

Satan's Strategy: The forces of darkness will cause division among the people of God in families, communities, and nations.

Satan's Tactic: Evil will incite and spread the spirits of pride, arrogance and defiance among God's children, and all of humanity.

Satan's Mission: Evil forces will work through man to destroy humanity, and win them to the side of evil. These forces will annihilate every man, woman, and child of God by preventing them from entering the light of eternity. They will be stripped of their God-given dignity, self-worth, and introduced to plans and tactics that will dethrone Gods credibility. The forces of evil will compel humanity to be lukewarm in their relationship with Jesus.

Considering this horrific mission, I need not explain in graphic detail the risks and dangers associated with connecting or dabbling in the world of darkness. There are frightening testimonies, further, stories from individuals who experienced profoundly devastating consequences after practicing rituals rooted in occultism or satanism. Sever yourself from all these activities. They originate from the underworld, and will lead to extreme confusion, evil, deprivation, severe suffering, deception, in some instances premature death, and even damnation.

We have both flesh and spirit, dark and light, in our visible and invisible world. Saint Paul in Corinthians shares about the nature of evil, and the legions of armies and rankings in the underworld. There are biblical truths about the nature of satan and the origins of sin and evil.

- Satan and his cohorts have existed since the beginning of time. Lucifer was present in the Garden of Eden with Adam and Eve and cast down to Earth after the great fall in the heavens.
- The origins of evil are deeply rooted in pride, rebellion, arrogance, jealousy, resistance, and defiance against the Creator.
- Sin issues are handed down through spiritual bloodlines, present in spiritual DNA, and show patterns in families over many generations.

- Sin and separation from God are part of our original human stain. Original sin stems from a nucleus of core sins discussed in this chapter.

- There are numerous levels of armies, and legions of demonic angels assigned to man by the prince of demons for different purposes.

- The overall duty of satan is to destroy God's love and light in man, deter the soul from receiving God's redemptive salvation, and steal us from the promise of heaven.

- The vision, mission, and tactics of satan discussed earlier in the chapter remain active until the moment we die.

- If satan can convince you that God does not exist, or he (satan) does not exist, his mission is accomplished.

- Satan is cunning, sly, manipulative and pervasive, spewing and whispering half-truths to deceive God's children.

- At times, satan will appear as an angel of light. Be on guard.

- It is possible even for those who preach, teach, and do good works to be deceived.

- Lucifer cannot read your mind; however, he can read actions, and circumstances in your life which he can then use to forge a plan to dismantle you in body, mind, and spirit.

- Satan looks for areas of weakness, vulnerability or woundedness in you, and then uses these liabilities as the open door to cripple and destroy your relationship with Christ, and others.

- Christians can be demonized (harassed), but cannot be embodied (demon possessed) by satan unless you grant permission. You are covered by the blood of Christ (His sacrificial death on the cross), but you still have free will.

- You are spiritually protected when you use the biblical armor of Christ (His word) under the authority of the blood covenant of Jesus.

- Demon possession exists. We have examples during the time of Christ until today.

- Warfare is real between demons and angelic hosts. This warring also can affect physical, spiritual, and earthly dimensions manifested by planetary and cosmic events.

Satan cowers, and runs from the power of God's authority and word. The light of Christ is a mighty double-edged sword that cuts satan to the quick and sends him running faster than a speeding bullet. Satan is bound and paralyzed from proceeding when Jesus's name and authority (through His blood covenant) is used and verbalized "out loud" by a righteous man or woman of God. Satan must still submit to God in the heavens.

Sin is active everywhere. It is present in individuals, collectively present in families, groups, politics, government, and even in the Church. Satan forges his greatest battleground of attack through the mind and heart of man.

Fortunately, humanity has inborn capacity to recognize evil, and even stronger spiritual capacity through God's grace to overcome, and reject it. Avoidance or refusal to sin is not contingent on emotion or feeling. It is based on a spiritual decision supported through grace, to maintain a consistent relationship with Christ to avoid sin and evil. Lucifer works through six major sin areas in man to destroy, divide, and conquer. These sin traps open the door, allow satan access, and give the devil ability to step inside and set up camp. The six major sins that set the trap, and allow him to enter are:

1. Offensiveness;
2. Pride;
3. Jealousy;
4. Deception;
5. Defiance, and
6. Arrogance.

Generational Strongholds

A stronghold is a barrier, wall, chain, or block which grips an individual, and prevents him or her from breaking free from a self-destructive pattern. Strongholds are based on deceptions, or falsehoods from the evil one, which can ultimately lead to serious offenses against God.

Generational strongholds handed down in families from generation to generation can include: violence, addictions, (drugs, sex, gambling, pornography), certain physical diseases, some forms of mental illness, occult practices (dabbling with mediums, ouija boards, witchcraft or the black arts) racial bigotry and prejudice.

Other vice-like grips can include: dominance and control, untimely deaths, physical or emotional trauma, extreme poverty, divorce or infidelity, sexual perversions, incest, polygamy, frequent accidents, discrimination, misogyny, unforgiveness, physical or sexual abuse, rejection, hatred, hexes or curses, abortion and sex slavery.

The Seventh Principle

You are empowered, protected, and delivered from situations which deny, attempt to destroy or diminish God's sovereignty in your life, through the power of Christ's superior blood covering.

"The weapons we fight with are not weapons of the world. On the contrary, they have divine power to demolish strongholds. We demolish arguments and every pretension that sets itself up against the knowledge of God, and we take captive every thought to make it obedient to Christ."

(2 Corinthians 10: V 4)

Three spiritual tactics that abolish evil, and securely position us in the protective heart of God are:

1. a humble and contrite spirit before the throne of God;
2. a spirit of daily repentance, and forgiveness of self and others; and
3. a willingness to grow spiritually by positioning oneself with the spirit of accountability through God's power in the Christian community (the people of God in the Church).

This means we should be teachable, accept constructive feedback, and spiritually appoint an individual other than our spouse or family member to help us stay on the straight and narrow.

Let Us Pray

Father,

I come before you with a heart that desires to receive all that you have for me. I ask you to reveal to me the areas in my life that have fallen short, the places inside my heart, mind, spirit or body that need to be transformed. Search me O Lord. Uncover, and reveal to me any sin or stronghold in my life that is preventing me from experiencing the fullness of Your power, healing, and transformation.

(Quiet yourself for fifteen minutes. Sit in an environment that is completely devoid of any extraneous sounds, distractions or "technical" noise. The Holy Spirit will reveal to you the areas He wants to bring to light. Feel free to write them down on a piece of paper).

Once the area(s) are revealed to you, repent and ask forgiveness.

Dear Lord,

I am truly sorry and ask forgiveness. Thank you for revealing these areas to me. I believe I am forgiven. I cast off every vain imagination, and now command it (them) captive and obedient to Christ. Give me Your grace and authority to break the power of sin and strongholds in my life forevermore. Grant me the courage to use Your covenant authority, so I do not repeat them again. I believe in faith, that I have received my rightful inheritance through salvation and a life-giving relationship with You. It is in You I trust. I am now delivered, forgiven, and pray I will be released evermore from the powers of sin and darkness in my life. Thank you, Lord. Amen.

CHAPTER SEVEN

Healing Rites of Passage Through Dreams, Visions, Prophecy and Praise

Despite the spiritual challenges we may encounter due to forces of evil in the world that I described in Chapter Six, God always sends divine consolations to support and uplift us.

These beautiful treasures of love, and solace come through dreams, visions, prophecies, and even our habits of prayerful praise before His throne. Let's take a closer look at how each of these fortify our spirit.

Before exploring dreams and visions generally, I'd like to begin this section by sharing an experience I had through a dream, which prepared me for the challenge of dealing with cancer.

Approximately five years before I started chemotherapy, I received a powerful message through a dream which I deeply cherish and will hold near to my heart for the remainder of my life.

During the night of the experience, I remember feeling exceptionally exhausted. I went to bed early and fell into a deep sleep. At some point in the sleep cycle I found myself outside my body, positioned in the upper regions of the universe among the stars. I was fully alert, awake, completely cognizant of my whereabouts, and instantly aware that I was in my spiritual body.

My nonphysical form was light, free, and floating, yet perfectly poised, and quietly suspended in my surroundings. I was perfectly aware of my spiritual essence; it felt natural, whole and complete. I was neither afraid or concerned, and completely at ease without any sense of evil or foreboding. I also felt keenly protected in my whereabouts, which was enveloped by a blanket of profound silence that felt soothing, and soulfully quieting. The impressions from my surroundings placed me all at once in a posture of expectancy and anticipation.

The experience persisted without any forced awareness of time or space, sensations of being encumbered, intimidated or frightened by the vastness of the universe which lay before me. It all seemed quite natural and easy. I remained poised for an encounter which I somehow already knew was going to take place.

Instantly, I recognized a powerful presence in my midst. I was aware beyond a shadow of a doubt that it was God. I could not "see" Him with my spiritual eyes, but I emphatically knew He was there. In fact, His presence was everywhere: powerful, permeating, all encompassing, commanding, magnificent, mighty, beyond spiritual awe, great, spiritually vast, phenomenally strong, constant, righteous, and supremely Holy. I also immediately knew I was personally known by Him.

Suddenly, He called my name, "M. . . . . . . a. . . . . . r. . . . . . y"

His voice was amazing. It seemed to move through space like a supersonic energy wave that struck my spiritual body instantly, sending shock waves throughout every cell in my spiritual form. The vibration from His voice passed through me, flooding me with divine impressions that were alive, musical, tingling, and pulsating. The sensations were swirling, vibrant, accompanied by energetic stirrings that were stunningly beautiful, thrilling, soul-rousing, immensely pleasurable, amazingly intense, and astonishing beyond words. No form of human communication could ever describe how exquisite this encounter was for me.

I could not measure how long I was out of my body during the experience, simply because there was seemingly no reference point or perceived need for time during the occurrence. After the encounter was finished, I slipped back into my body—which was like reentering into a heavy cast iron box—and opened my eyes with complete awareness of the occurrence. The encounter was incredible and mind-boggling. It left such an indelible imprint on my soul that no one could ever convince me that it was merely a fanciful dream.

God is not only real, He is vastly POWERFUL, beyond words! His actual word creates and brings forth life. John I: V I states:

"In the beginning was the Word, and the Word was with God, and the Word was God."

The experience convinced me that:

1. God absolutely exists, and always has. He is real, not some figment of our imagination. His word stirs, and powerfully creates all on its own.

2. There are no words to describe His sovereignty. It is immense, holy, astronomical, magnificent, phenomenal, and endless beyond words. Nothing compares to it, and nothing ever will.

3. False gods (deities), or entities worshipped by nations or peoples of Earth are pure folly in comparison to the vast, and endless existence of this Holy Being. He is beyond measure. Nothing on Earth, absolutely no deity, no god compares to this loving, all-encompassing, astonishing Being we call our "Father."

4. He knows each of us personally (it's so incredible) and calls us each by name.

5. We have spiritual form or palpable essence (presence) after death. We shed our confining, limiting, heavy encasement of flesh, purposed to serve us only for a time, and season on Earth. Our spiritual form is free, light, and perfectly aware. It is like having a third eye. Everything is remarkably clear and known in an instant. Movement and sounds are likened to ripples of energy waves which move quicker than the speed of light or sound in our dimension.

6. Our spiritual form contains an identifiable personality which is self-recognizable, and completely known to God. During the experience, I was able to recognize myself in spiritual form. My identity was not hidden from me in my spiritual body.

7. The spiritual body is protected as a child of God, and in a state of knowing when it is released from the flesh. Transitioning from flesh to spirit is painless and easy. The spirit literally slips out of the body without effort or pain, as if it is summoned by God and responds, or simply is aware that it is time to go.

8. We immediately identify God in our non-physical state. There is no mistaking Him, whether you believe He exists or not.

Finally, my experience was confirmed through three scriptures:

1. John I: V I shares that the spoken word from God is not only powerful, it has the phenomenal ability to stir, create and bring forth life.

    And God said, "Let there be light," and there was light."
    (Genesis I: V 3)

2. 2 Corinthians 5: V 8 shares about our confidence that when we are away from the body, we are in the presence of the Lord.

3. Isaiah 43: V I assures us that as children of God, we are each called by name:

    "Fear not, for I have redeemed you; I have summoned you by name; you are mine."

As I reflect on the relevance, and timing of the experience, God bestowed a powerful message of comfort, and encouragement in me which affirmed He was with me, and vowed His love for me more than I could ever believe possible. This prepared me for my future trial with cancer, and planted in me a spirit of hope and faith, despite the challenges I encountered during the period of my delayed healing. I believe that in this moment God also called me to a new mission.

Isaiah 43: V 2 - 3 states,

"When you pass through the waters, I will be with you; and when you pass through the rivers, they will not sweep over you. When you walk through the fire, you will not be burned; the flames will not set you ablaze. For I am the Lord, your God, the Holy One of Israel, your Savior;"

Dreams and Visions

God speaks to us through dreams, and visions to encourage us, transform and renew our mind and spirit. We are told in Joel 2: V 28:

> "And afterward, I will pour out my Spirit on all people. Your sons and daughters will prophesy, your old men will dream dreams, your young men will see visions. Even on my servants, both men and women, I will pour out my Spirit in those days"

Throughout the Old and New Testament, God spoke to the very heart and soul of humanity though dreams and visions to bring relief, comfort, and provide wisdom, and direction to His people. Do we have to be suspicious of our dreams, discount or discard them?

We must use spiritual caution when interpreting our dreams. Some dreams may originate simply from the activities of the day, or the world, flesh or devil. How then do we affirm whether a dream experience is from God, from self or perpetuated by evil? It is important to test your dream against scripture and evaluate the fruit it produces in your life.

If you receive spiritual direction through a dream (a sleeping message) or vision (a waking dream or mental image that's seen with the mind's eye or human eye), and it is Godly, spiritually grounded, confirmed through scripture, confirmed through members in the Church as being authentic, gives you clarity of mind, and draws you closer to God and others, it is most likely from the spirit of God. Additionally, if it proves true for your circumstance, you can be sure the dream or vision is founded in the heart of God and sent to you for a specific purpose.

If a dream is frightening, leaves you confused, upset, bewildered, causes you to sin or urges you to seek a medium or dabble in the dark arts for interpretation, the dream is not from God. If a dream reinforces a mental delusion or hallucination, it is a unfounded, contorted message which holds no connection or bearing to Christ, and most likely is rooted in the strongholds of chemical or mental illness.

How do our dreams connect with rites of healing?

Sometimes, God will send a message in a dream or vision as an invitation, reminder, warning or share future events that hold important meaning for your life. These dreams or images will bring a specific revelation, direction, or help you make a Godly decision. Often, these messages ultimately bring a greater awareness of God's presence in your life, or special healing in body, mind or spirit.

In the Old Testament, God shared with Abraham (through a dream) that he would become the father of all nations and have a son. However, God did not reveal the timetable in Earth years as to when that would happen. Abraham believed in faith against all odds that he and his wife, Sarah, would bear a child in their later years. They did. God sent a dream to Abimelech urging him to leave Sarah alone, because she was the wife of Abraham (even though Abraham had told Abimelech that Sarah was his sister). God sent a dream to Joseph, revealing that his family would one day bow before him (they did years later in Egypt, but not before Joseph was thrown into a pit by his jealous brothers when he shared the dream, then enslaved by Pharaoh, and assumed dead by Joseph's father). The Pharaoh of Egypt was given a dream by God, so that Joseph could interpret it. This ultimately won him favor with the king. When Joseph interpreted the dream, warning Pharaoh about seasons that would occur both with harvest and drought in Egypt, he was chosen to serve next to him, in a high position in his court.

In the New Testament, Zacharias dreamed he would bear a son who would prepare the way for the savior. This was John the Baptist. Ananias was instructed in a vision to visit Saul in Damascus, and speak a word given to him by God to reverse his blindness. Mary the mother of God received a vision that she would become the mother of Jesus even though she was still a virgin. Joseph was warned in a dream to flee to Egypt, and take Jesus and Mary away from Herod, a powerful governor who ruled at the time of Jesus's birth. He heard about the birth of Jesus, and his future kingship among the Jewish people. He sought to destroy Jesus by issuing a decree to kill all the first-born males in the region.

God is not bound by time or conditions when He chooses to speak to us through dreams, or visions to accomplish His plans and purposes.

Prophecy

The gift of prophecy is a word of knowledge only God can reveal to us. This word, which is directly spoken by God can be channeled through an individual with the gift of prophetic stirrings.

The gift, which is recognized in scripture, is affirmed as an authentic message from God which holds great significance. It is one method among many which God uses to bring hope to His people, through forewarnings or powerful communications which communicate comfort, instruction or healing. The prophecy given me the night of the healing service was a confirmation the Lord not only heard my prayer for healing but answered it in accordance with His will for my life. His message was clear. I would recover despite the challenges I would encounter, and live long years.

In the Old and New Testament, God used the prophets, and His son Jesus to speak words of prophecy, warn or protect people from danger, share revelation, impart correction or uplift the weary or sick. Prophecy is still prevalent in the Church today. It is a source of great reassurance from God, both individually and collectively, bringing a deep sense of encouragement and healing.

When a word of prophecy is spoken to an individual, it quickens the heart, impresses truth on the soul, imparts knowledge, and uplifts the spirit of the person receiving it.

Jeremiah 33: V 3 shares how God discloses His word to us.

"Call to me and I will answer you and tell you great and unsearchable things you do not know."

I encourage you to pray and seek God's prophetic word. Encourage the gift of prophecy in your Church through your clergy and pastors, or members of your congregation. God does not lie. Confirm the prophetic word through scripture, evaluate the fruit it bears in your life, and the collective life of the Church. If you receive a specific word, and the confirmation from God which states you will be healed, then believe it. You WILL be healed!

A Prophetic Word

"My child I love you with an everlasting love. Do not be afraid. I am aware of every circumstance in your life and have heard your prayer. I have called you by name, you are mine. Receive My love, My grace and My strength to sustain you. Walk in My peace and My wisdom to guide you. My ways are not your ways, My purposes are not your purposes. Trust me. I will provide you with everything you need to fortify and strengthen you. Your thoughts will become My thoughts. My heart will become your heart. I am your Father and you are My child. Accept My grace as you bathe in My love and rest in the plans and path I have for you.

The power of My mighty right hand is upon you. Receive this power in all its fullness, for My healing, My love, My Holy Spirit and unending Mercy is given freely to all who ask. In every moment, praise Me for all that I am doing in your life. You are My child. I love you."

Praise

There are over sixty verses in scripture which declare the spiritual benefits of praise to God despite our circumstances.

Praise is not only a form of worship which is pleasing to God, it is your mustard seed of faith which proclaims His greatness and releases power and grace into your situation—which in turn, brings healing and transformation.

> "Through Jesus, therefore, let us continually offer to God a sacrifice of praise—the fruit of lips that confess his name."
> (Hebrews 13: V 15)

Below are a series of powerful praises based upon scripture to resurrect, transform, and renew your mind. If you place yourself under the mighty covenant of Christ through praise, God will act accordingly, righteously, and lovingly to save, and heal you.

1. I praise You with my heart and lips O Lord, even though I do not understand my present situation.
2. I will sing a song of praise to You and continue to believe that You are sovereign over my situation, Jesus, despite what I see in the natural.
3. I will praise You as I call to You, knowing You will answer my plea for help, comfort, and for healing. Save me, O Lord, and I will be saved.
4. I praise you, God, as You fulfill your purpose in me, even as I am enduring this trial.
5. I praise You, Jesus. I am fearfully and wonderfully made by You. You know every inch of me, and every hair on my head. I praise You in advance for Your course-correction in my body, mind, and spirit.
6. I will praise You when I am awake, I will praise You when I am asleep, and even in my dreams, I will think of you, for I love you, O God.
7. I praise You Jesus for hearing my request and answering it in accordance with Your perfect plan for my life.

Powerful Affirmations

The word of God cuts to the chase. It's a double-edged sword that brings healing into every area of your life. It can empower, illuminate, and fortify you in your darkest hour. There are one-hundred and fifty Psalms in the New International Version of the Bible (NIV) that can literally change the course of your spiritual and earthly destiny. We are told in scripture, to be transformed by the renewing of our minds. (Romans 12: V 2)

As you repeat these twenty-one affirmations based on the Psalms daily, I declare under the authority of Christ, that you *will* receive healing in mind, body and spirit, and share powerful testimony of God's unfailing love, and mercy in your life.

> **Affirmation One (Psalm I: V I - 6)**
> I will change my way of thinking, believe in you, delight in your law O God, and trust that my life will yield blessing in the appointed season.

Affirmation Two (Psalm 2: V 1 - 12)
Jesus, I proclaim you as Lord over my life.

Affirmation Three (Psalm 3: V 1 - 8)
God, I believe you can and do protect me from those who seek to hurt me. I am delivered by you.

Affirmation Four (Psalm 4: V 1 - 8)
I believe You are a God of mercy. I have been set apart, and trust You have my best interest in mind.

Affirmation Five (Psalm 5: V 1 - 12)
I love Your name, Jesus! Thank you for Your protection, and favor in my life.

Affirmation Six (Psalm 6: V 1 - 10)
Lord, thank You for hearing my request, and answering my prayer for healing.

Affirmation Seven (Psalm 7: V 1 - 17)
You are a watchful God: I believe You protect me against the snares of evil.

Affirmation Eight (Psalm 8: V 1 - 9)
You have placed upon me honor, favor and blessing. Lord, I am indebted to You. Your powerful hand intervenes for me daily.

Affirmation Nine (Psalm 9: V 1 - 20)
Lord, You are for me, and not against me. You hear my cause, and I declare Your sovereignty over my situation. I have faith, and confidence in You.

Affirmation Ten (Psalm 10: V 1 - 18)
I cast off every sin and vain imagination that steers me away from Your power working in my life.

Affirmation Eleven (Psalm 11: V 1 - 7)

I know that vengeance is Yours, O God. I place in Your hands those who seek to hurt, malign, gossip against me, or smear my life. I declare Your ability to free me from this oppression and stronghold once, and for all.

Affirmation Twelve (Psalm 12: V 1 - 8)

Take control over my tongue, words and speech, Lord. Help me not to curse or judge others but bless them.

Affirmation Thirteen (Psalm 13: V 1 - 6)

Lord, I choose to be redeemed. Do not allow me to be snatched away by satan but free me through the power of Your redemption. Show me how to overcome the enemy in my life. I trust in Your unfailing love for me, and ability to rescue me from my enemies.

Affirmation Fourteen (Psalm 14: V 1 - 7)

Lord, I believe you are who you say you are. You are the great I AM. I place my cares, and situation into Your capable hands.

Affirmation Fifteen (Psalm 15: V 1 - 5)

Help me Father, I need to control my thought life. Give me grace. I do not want to cast the first stone, but only seek forgiveness for my own faults and sin.

Affirmation Sixteen (Psalm 16: V 1 - 11)

Jesus, I believe You will never abandon me or give me anything too hard to bare. Thank you for surrounding me with your unfailing love and protection. I am safe and secure under Your refuge. Your Godly boundaries encircle my life.

Affirmation Seventeen (Psalm 17: V 1 - 15)

Give me strength when I am put to the test, Lord. Save me from myself, and the enemy.

Affirmation Eighteen (Psalm 18: V 1 - 50)

Lord, You are my rock, my strength, and my help when I am in trouble. Whom should I fear?

Affirmation Nineteen (Psalm 19: V 1 - 9)

I proclaim Your powerful work O Lord in my life. There is no one mightier than You. You know the secret desires of my heart.

Affirmation Twenty (Psalm 20: V 1 - 9)

Thank you, Lord, for granting my requests for healing in accordance with Your will for my life.

Affirmation Twenty-One (Psalm 21: V 1 - 13)

Thank you, Lord, for giving me the desires of my heart. I will sing your praises and testify to Your name.

CHAPTER EIGHT

Let the Victory Dance Begin!

If you've completed reading *The Victory Dance of God*, you are now ready to receive the healing that God has for you.

As you begin these series of prayers, I proclaim, and declare the covenant of God's healing power to rain over you in the name of Jesus. His promise is rightfully yours as a child of God. May He manifest in your life the fullness of His love, release you from the power of death; free you from mental, spiritual, and bodily illness, and reawaken in you, His light and healing in accordance with His word, and superior blood covenant.

My Pledge of Faith

I will receive every good gift from the Lord. It will be poured into my life because of His great love for me. For the measure I have in faith, will be given to me as a blessing according to His plans and purposes for healing in my body, mind, and spirit through His son, Jesus. Amen.

I encourage you to recite the prayers of deliverance that follow on the next few pages, *"out loud"* as often as you need or feel led to. Share them with your loved ones, with your Church life groups, at Church functions or when you are in a situation that requires urgent intercession. Let the Holy Spirit guide and answer you according to His plans and purposes for your life. May each petition go up as incense before His throne. I pray that the anointing of the Holy Spirit will be manifested in power over you, and ask God to bless your requests and use them for His honor and glory.

Prayers of Deliverance

Prayer of Release from Mental Aberrations and Psychological Conditions

Scripture confirms we are to be of sound mind. God does not give us the spirit of depression, fear, anxiety, panic, compulsiveness, rage, agitation, rebellion, paranoia, or schizophrenia.

Neither does He send us the spirit of suspiciousness, offensiveness, nervousness, grandiosity, doublemindedness, delusional thoughts, violence, thoughts to harm others or self, mania, accusatory or judgmental spirits, angry or hostile spirits, spirits of hallucinations, prejudice, rejection, hostility, bitterness, dominance, arrogance, entitlement, selfishness, hatred, manipulation or unforgiveness. These temperaments, thoughts and mental aberrations are foreign to the spirit of God, and can be loosed from the mind through the power of Christ who severs and cancels mental strongholds. If you are plagued by one or any of these disturbances:

Pray Your Prayer of Mental Release

God has established in me a sound mind. I therefore release myself, in the name of Jesus, from all thoughts emanating in my mind, emotions or spirit that are foreign to the character of God, especially notions which keep me prisoner or vulnerable to powers of the underworld. I now claim these strongholds forever subject to the superior blood of Christ. I command that every vain imagination, every twisted or aberrant thought be taken captive, and obedient to the light of Jesus. I free myself from these temperaments now, in the present realm, and forevermore. I claim over me, in me and through me, the deliverance of Christ from these mental strongholds. I cast His bright light into every corner of my mind, and spirit. I pour the blood of Christ on every mental disturbance, whether caused by chemical imbalances in my brain or those emanating from an ill heart or spirit. I command in confidence through Christ, that ALL of them be severed, and released never to return, in the authority of Jesus.

I am now free, unshackled, and fully present to the power of Jesus's death and resurrection working in my heart, mind, and spirit in this moment. His light now surrounds and hedges a protective shield around me. I affirm, and declare that nothing may enter my heart, spirit or touch my mind that is not of God. I claim and authorize these aberrations of mind, and spirit released by the word of Christ, the supremacy and power of Jesus working in me, and the shield of His blood which now covers me forevermore. It is in His (Jesus's) name I say Amen.

Prayer to Discern and Release Spiritual Attacks and Assaults

Whenever God is working powerfully in your life, expect opposition to follow. It is common for the forces of evil to harass, attack, or attempt to spiritually, physically or mentally thwart the will, plans and purposes of God in you.

These attacks can manifest in the form of illness, job loss, betrayal, relational division, rejection, hostility against you, false judgement, financial loss, family strife, tragedy or other devastating events sent to test or defeat your spiritual relationship with Jesus. They can also turn your heart away from the Church, incite a spirit of hopelessness, defeat or judgement of others in you, or even provoke the spirit of condemnation against the very people who love you, and who love God. It is important to recognize these attacks as enemies of Christ. They will attempt to rob you of your spiritual vitality, break your trust relationship with Jesus, and remove His abiding peace in you.

However, God's power is greater in you than the evil that influences our flesh, and the world. Further, you possess the effective weapon of prayer, and the authority of Christ to smash these attacks because of the act of His redemption. You are fully armed and equipped!

You will recognize the onslaughts of spiritual attacks or assaults from the enemy when these attitudes of the spirit begin creeping into your life.

1. You begin to feel a sense of doom and gloom, as if you can't "get out from under."
2. You begin to focus more on your troubles than you do on God's power to deliver you.
3. Your prayer life diminishes, or you begin to separate yourself from the Christian community.
4. You start to adopt a spirit of complaint against God, rather than a spirit of praise to God.
5. You begin to judge members in (and of) your Church, or adopt a self-righteous attitude that creates complacency, division or discord in your heart or spirit.
6. The Word of God does not console or strengthen you anymore.
7. You readjust and unknowingly adopt the spirit of the world rather than seek the spirit, and strength of Christ within you.
8. You begin to have difficulty praying for God's guidance, comfort and wisdom.

In the book of Job, we are warned of a Leviathan spirit who is deceptive and cunning. Specifically, in Job 41: V 1 - 34, the bible describes this vile spirit in detail. It states that his breath sets coals ablaze, and flame's dart from its mouth. This spirit especially fastens itself to those who are proud of heart. Because of the powerful influence of the Leviathan spirit, which is deceptive and cunning, hardness of heart not only consumes an individual, but can even cause them to break from the Church.

Pray Your Prayer of Release from Spiritual Attacks and Assaults (The Leviathan Spirit)

I approach the throne of God the Father, His Son and Holy Spirit believing that the power of the Trinity and saints of God are intervening for me in this moment. I know the battle of the enemy is real, but the strength of Christ, and His superior blood covenant is greater. I repent Lord, of the sin of pride. I command the warring angels of God to defend me in battle, and destroy every spiritual assault, attack on my life, and my family's life in the name of Jesus. In the authority of Christ's name, I sever and cancel every plot, plan, evil intent, or spiritual onslaught placed upon me, and those I love through any person, place, event or situation by this spirit. I authorize a holy hedge of protection around me against the powers of darkness. I now break the spirit of Leviathan in my life in the name of Jesus. I place an angelic army of light around me to fight my battles. I declare that nothing outside the will of God will touch, harm or destroy me, as I place Christ's protective mantle over me, and the lives of those I love. Through the power of the Holy Spirit I activate in the spiritual realm, His powerful plans and purposes for my life and claim a reaping of blessing upon my head in the earthly realm. I firmly believe the battle is won. I await full manifestation of the fruits of the Holy Spirit made manifest in my life, and flesh. May the bearing of this fruit, reconnect me to the Church, and the people of God. In Jesus's name. Amen.

Prayer to Release Soul Ties, Violence and Abuse

We live in a world where violence is real. Sexual, mental, physical, emotional, and verbal abuse is rampant. These ugly spirits manifest themselves in many different forms directly or indirectly through murder, rape, violence, molestation, mental abuse, or injustice against women, children of both genders, and other vulnerable members of society. They leave emotional scarring, and fear in their wake. This can traumatically tie an individual to their emotional experience over the course of a life time.

There are at least forty-five verses in the bible which address the spirit of violence. In Ezekiel 7: V 23, we learn that these spirits of violence are nothing new. They were present and known even to the apostles, and followers of Christ, thousands of years ago.

> ". . . because the land is full of bloodshed and the city is full of violence."

These vile spirits continue to be present even more so today—especially in godless countries—where men, women, and children are experiencing the maniacal fury of demonic activity. It is in these times the Church as the "hope and light of the world," is appointed to rise against these evil injustices. United prayer, consistent fasting, and use of the authority of Christ against these principalities can defeat them.

Pray the Prayer of Release from Soul Ties, Violence and Abuse

I approach the throne of God with a heart of repentance for anything that I have said in thought, word or deed which has opened the door to spirits of violence, abuse, or any painful unrighteous soul tie(s) I have brought against myself, or others have brought against me, (through these activities), that cannot seemingly be broken. Specifically, I renounce all forms of hatred, judgement, division, bigotry, loathing, mental or spiritual violation I have visited upon others. I also release and forgive any violence or abuse others have visited upon me through their speech, or held me captive, through their direct, or indirect actions. I break these strongholds, and soul ties over me in the name of Jesus. I ask the Holy Spirit to cleanse and repair the aftermath of these actions that have hurt me, in the powerful name, and blood of Jesus. I sever all forms of abuse from others. I renounce any self-abuse caused by the sin(s) of gluttony, sexual immorality, sexual promiscuity or impurity, self-hatred, self-rejection or self-harm. I now command these spirits to leave now and forevermore, never to return.

I plead, under the superior blood of Christ, for the disarming and annihilation of the spirit of violence or abuse through my generational blood lines, which may have manifested itself against me, or other members in my family blood lines. I declare spiritual protection, and pray for the release of myself, family, and even states, and nations of the world from maniacal spirits who commit acts of violence or abuse against humanity. I bind them up now with the mighty, spiritual blood-cord of Christ, break their grip—and place them powerless at the foot of the cross. I authorize their disposal in accordance with the justice and supremacy of Christ. I call forth a mantle of peace, protection of warring angels, and the love of Jesus to replace, cover over, and fill the empty spaces. I declare and claim this action complete as a child of God and expect the full manifestation of this prayer in faith to be binding upon myself, and all hearts and minds, people, and lands for Christ. In Jesus's name. Amen.

Prayer to Release Generational and Individual Strongholds

Strongholds are present in families and individuals. They are repetitive sin patterns or behaviors which hold individuals or family members hostage over generations. They can be categorized as physical, mental or spiritual.

How do you know whether your family or you are under a stronghold? What are the signs? For something to constitute a stronghold, it must meet one, some, or all four of the following criteria:

1. It asserts influential control over your life or family and overpowers your will to resist it.
2. It constitutes a repetitive behavior that not only holds you, and your family hostage, but it is a pattern from which you cannot break free.
3. It presents itself as a physical, mental or spiritual aberration which places you or your family in a position of bondage.
4. It causes you or your family mental, spiritual or physical harm, which reaps suffering rather than healing, and blessing.

There are numerous types of physical strongholds. Physical strongholds can manifest through familial generations of same-type diseases or events such as: cancers, genetic abnormalities, accidents, untimely deaths, family traumas, miscarriages, obesity, addictions, heart disease, liver disease, and other generational patterns handed down through family bloodlines.

Mental strongholds include forms of mental illness or behavioral patterns which can manifest in families over generations. Bigotry, hatred, divorce, and marital infidelity, incest, molestation, twisted mental patterns, addictions, forms of schizophrenia, doublemindedness, suicide, mania, self-harm, homicidal behavior, cruelty toward persons or animals, self-accusation, grandiosity, depression, mania, rage, paranoia, unfounded suspiciousness, compulsiveness, and mental obsessions are all such strongholds.

Sexual strongholds in generations can include repetitive sin patterns or sexual deviances which manifest as; infidelity, incest, lust, pornography, sexual abominations, sexual molestation, twisted sex, polygamy, sexual promiscuity or sensual-sexual peculiarities. Spiritual strongholds can appear as stealing, lying, cursing, obsessive-compulsive behaviors, fascination with the occult, satanism, witchery or religious practices rooted in the dark arts.

Pray the Prayer of Release from Generational or Individual Strongholds

I release myself from every generational, and individual stronghold that plagues me (name it/them), in the name of Jesus. I release its power over me, its ability to tempt me, and my inability to resist it. I break its dominion over me, and free myself from its grip by the superior blood covenant of Jesus Christ. I unshackle and break its chain around my neck. I release its clutch on me, my family, and generational blood lines. I declare complete freedom in the name of Jesus, and command this/these stronghold(s) be placed before the throne of God to be disposed of in accordance with the justice and righteousness of Christ. I command them never to return in my life or the lives of my family or loved ones again, in Jesus's name. Amen.

Prayer to Release Medical and Physical Disorders

If you are struggling with a medical or physical disorder, you are not alone. We live in a fallen world subject to dis-ease in our bodies. Human disorders are endless, despite the valiant attempts of science, and medicine to cure them.

Dis-ease can take the form of biological disorders which cause discomfort, pain and severe distress. God is not only aware of your suffering. Your suffering is fully known to Him. He is sovereign over all of it. Every malady, ailment, condition, sickness or syndrome is understood by Him, followed by the ultimate power and authority to deliver, repair, restore, renew, make whole, and transform you through one of the four channels we discussed early on in my book, which best serves your life, and situation. You need only believe that He is working for your highest good. Trust His path. Remain confident that His course of action is perfect, and purposed just for you. Ultimately, God will always provide a way out. This is scriptural. He will open every door that needs to open. He will also shut every door you are not destined to walk through during the period of dis-ease. He *will heal you* either through the supernatural, miraculous, extraordinary or the ordinary.

> "And we know that in all things God works for the good of those who love him, who have been called according to his purpose."
>
> (Romans 8: V 28)

When you pray for healing, here is a way to approach the throne of God:

1. Begin with a word of praise and thanks.
2. Ask forgiveness for anything you have done in thought, word or deed which has separated you from Christ.
3. Place your specific request(s) before Him.
4. Thank Him in advance for the outcome. In doing so, you release His power and promise to heal and equip you, provide Godly strength, infuse supernatural wisdom, and ultimately provide everything you need to sustain you beyond your limited resources and inability to cope.

Pray the Prayer for Release of Your Medical or Physical Condition

Father, I approach your throne in a spirit of praise and thanksgiving for Your love, protection, favor, and grace in my life. I thank You for all the times You have rescued me and spared my life from danger. Without You, I am nothing. Save me O God. I ask forgiveness for the times I separated myself from Your steadfast love and mercy, refused your direction, or guidance from the Holy Spirit.

I need Your help. I need Your healing. I need Your protection. I place before You my condition. I simply ask, will You completely heal me of this (name the condition or illness)? I request this in faith, knowing that my healing is underserved. I ask in the name of the sacrifice, love and saving grace of Your son Jesus, who stands before You, and intercedes on my behalf. I place myself completely in Your hands through faith, trusting that Your timing, and path is perfect, and plan and purpose will unfold in due season. I know all things are possible with You. I thank You in advance for this healing, which is now complete in the divine, and manifested in the fullness of my flesh, and spirit according to Your perfect will through the supernatural, miraculous, extraordinary or ordinary. Protect and instruct me, give me patience and perseverance while You unfold and reveal Your plan to heal me. I will testify to Your greatness and give You thanks and praise, in the name of your son, Jesus. Amen.

Prayer to Release Addictions

Addiction is a form of enslavement of the body, mind, or spirit which holds an individual hostage, making him or her a slave or dependent on a stimulus, action or object which robs them of their God-given right to live in mental, spiritual, and physical freedom.

Addictions occur in many different forms:

1. Drugs;
2. Sex;

3. Food;
4. Gambling;
5. Tobacco;
6. Self-destructive or obsessive habits;
7. Pornography;
8. Work;
9. Social Media;
10. Money;
11. Status and power;
12. Sex; and
13. Material things.

There are two stages of an addiction:

First Stage - A compelling force (either as a temptation of the flesh or evil persuasion) is introduced to an individual beyond their human capacity to resist. Once the person succumbs to the lure, and accepts the bait, the second stage is triggered.

Second Stage - A forceful, unrelenting physical and/or mental urge then overtakes the individual, seducing the individual or provoking him or (her) to continue with the behavior. It convinces the person into believing he or (she) cannot live without it. This fuels the addiction, making it difficult to break the chain, or circle of repetition without spiritual or physical intervention.

Pray the Prayer of Release from the Spirit of Addiction

Father, I come to you today in a spirit of desperation, with a humble, and contrite heart. I seek your help, and deliverance from a force inside me which is greater than my will or power to resist.

I am addicted to (name it). I come before Your throne and plead Your powerful intervention in this matter. I ask that You sever and eliminate it from my life. I beseech the superior blood of Christ over me, in me, and through me. I reject the grip of this powerful stronghold which places a chain around my neck and keeps me hostage from having a spirit-filled relationship with You. You are greater in me than the addiction which seeks to destroy me, and the lives of those around me. I repent. Thank You for this deliverance. I accept Your divine intervention now, and the help from those around me, for my restoration in body, mind, and spirit. Thank you for Your Divine power to help me resist this compulsion now, and forevermore. I declare myself free, loosed, and emancipated from this addiction. I affirm that this dependency, and my need for it, will immediately depart, never to return. It is in the name of Jesus, and the authority of His word I pray and say, Amen.

Prayer to Release Depression and the Spirit of Self-Destruction

The root cause of depression, in many cases, is often unjustified anger against oneself or another, which is turned inward. Depression or hopelessness, is counter to the Spirit of God. He is a Father of comfort, encouragement and hope. He also gives us a spirit of worth through His son Jesus, who is the giver of divine love, confidence, contentment and peace. All these fruits are available to each of us through His loving, powerful, Holy Spirit.

We are all immensely loved by our Father, who supplies all our needs through Christ Jesus, His beloved Son. When His love is in us, it is enough.

Pray the Prayer of Release from Depression

Father, I come before you feeling hopeless, depressed, and despondent, not knowing how to elevate my soul or spirit. I long to participate in life in all its fullness, with joy, peace, and hope for a future filled with joy-filled possibilities. I long to be in the mainstream of Your holy and tender plans you've fashioned just for me. In the name of Jesus, I release myself from the spirit of depression, and request through your blood covenant with me, that it be replaced with the spirit of joy. Please heal the root of my depression, bring it into the light, and transform it for Your honor and glory. I pray for men and women of "Godly" intent to support me in prayer, and guide me into solid counsel so that I may reap the benefits of a joy-filled life that has always been destined for me since the beginning of time. It's in your powerful name I pray and say Amen.

Pray the Prayer of Release from the Spirit of Self-Harm

Suicide is pervasive in our culture, especially with young people. Self-destruction, or the act of destroying oneself through behaviors that are pitted against one's own body, or killing oneself, in the name of despair, are actions that deeply affect the heart of God because He loves us so much. These actions also profoundly affect and wound the hearts of those who are left behind.

God's love for you is tender, compassionate, and full of mercy. It is filled with fresh, new grace-filled moments each day. The promises He gives us in His word are true. He will never leave us or forsake us. Further, He will never give us anything too hard to bear without a way of support, intervention, or godly way of escape. The power of His divine grace, and love is sufficient. When we attempt to hurt or harm ourselves, or "snuff" our lives' out in an act of self-desperation or self-will, (whether we are cognizant of our actions or not), we close ourselves off from the redeeming and restorative power that Jesus has to offer as the hope and light of the world. He is always ready, willing and able to divinely intervene on our behalf. The decision or temptation to commit suicide, never emanates from our Heavenly Father. It is contrary to the nature of God to tempt us to harm ourselves in an act of desperation or self-destruction. These feelings or expressions of suicide, demand immediate attention, as well as spiritual, and professional intervention.

Pray the Prayer of Release from Self-Harm

Jesus, I approach your throne in the spirit of utter despair. I am having feelings that are pressing me, to end my life. I know these thoughts are not rooted in your loving, merciful, and tender heart, or your divine nature to heal and restore me, no matter how desperate or intense my situation seems right now. I therefore, take this leap of faith, and ask you to rescue me in this moment. Break and demolish, through the power of your Holy Spirit, the spirit of suicide in me. Sever the compulsion to want to kill myself. I believe this thought is not from You. Restore me emotionally, through the power of Your grace. Help me to bring this declaration into the light, with someone I know, and or trust. Rescue me from these disturbing thoughts O God, and free me to live a life filled with hope, and love in YOU. I take these thoughts captive, and obedient to Christ and place them before the throne to be disposed of in accordance with Your perfect will for my life. Guide me to strong, professional, spirit-led counsel, and knit me back together again in body, mind, and spirit. I pray this prayer, in the mighty name of Jesus; my rock, deliverer and ever-present fortress in need. Amen.

Prayer to Release the Powers of the Occult

There are Christians knowingly and unknowingly involved in the occult. These activities are introduced as "fun," or practiced on a frequent basis due to curiosity or belief in their power.

Scripture warns about these activities which open the door to the underworld. Occult practices include:

1. superstitious beliefs, or notions of one having psychic abilities or special powers;
2. practice of witchcraft, sorcery, voodoo, wizardry, magic;
3. astrology;
4. divination, entertaining evil visitations, clairvoyance, or use of mediums to predict the future;
5. blood covenants; and/or
6. satanic worship.

Christ speaks to us through prophecy, dreams and visions. These gifts are given to us through channels of *His divine light* which fortify, strengthen, and heal us.

Occult experiences (seeing ghosts, going to mediums, having the dead communicate through séances or using tarot cards to contact the dead), originate from the underworld, and can open the door to satanic strongholds which invite danger, suffering, pain, tragedy, disaster, and even death in some circumstances; both individually or collectively. If you are involved in occult practices directly or indirectly, discontinue these activities now, in the name of Jesus.

Pray the Prayer of Release from the Occult

In the name, and in the blood of Jesus, I place myself at the foot of the cross, and request to be liberated from the desire to engage in or involve myself with occult practices. Lord, please forgive me for participating in these activities. I sever and cancel, in the name of Jesus, my fascination with the satanic arts. I remove, under the blood of Christ, all curses, hexes, jinxes, enchantments, spells or bewitchments cast upon me, from activities in which I participated, knowingly or unknowingly. I encircle myself in the divine light of Christ, and call upon Your intervention, Jesus, for the release from their influence, and grip that have been placed upon me from the underworld, and in which I have also knowingly or unknowingly placed upon myself. I seek Your protection, and healing. I request the Holy Spirit, Michael the Archangel, and all the angelic hosts as Christ's guardians to break this preoccupation, curiosity and involvement with the occult. I place the hedge of Christ's light around me, as I disengage, break every tie, and cut every association with the underworld and occult arts. Take up my battle for me, through the blood of Jesus. Safeguard and encamp around me. I seek repentance and ask for Your mercy, love, and power to rebuild my faith and confidence in YOU, forevermore. I plead never to participate in these activities again. In Jesus's name, I believe. Amen.

Prayer to Release the Powers of Bigotry, Prejudice and Discrimination

God created each of us to fit into a beautiful divine tapestry of colors and cultures which reflect His infinite creativity, and love for all humankind.

We are endowed with different gifts, and talents that fit into the fabric of humanity for a reason and purpose.

Cultural privilege, separation, oppression, and segregation are strongholds that arise from our fallen (sin) nature. They are pervasive both in men, women, and all races, and cultures throughout the world. They originate from the sins of pride and arrogance, leaving harm, mental enslavement, woundedness, and oppression in their wake. God created each of us differently to be celebrated, loved, accepted, and joined together in a state of spiritual unity, and interdependence—not division. Racial discrimination and bigotry is widespread throughout the world, and used by satan to create hostility, aggression, gender bias, violence, murder, and division between races. It requires deliverance on an individual and collective level.

Pray the Prayer of Release from Bigotry, Prejudice and Discrimination

In the name of Jesus, and the power of His superior blood covenant, I release myself from all thoughts or actions that entertain or foster deceptive notions of superiority, privilege or special benefit that I believe are deserved or justified. I cancel and sever all thoughts, vain imaginations, or false notions that create sinful judgement or division against individuals or groups that I may think of as different from me. I release every judgement I have made against humanity that was rooted in the sins of prejudice, fear, hatred, arrogance, division, pride or racial discrimination. I sever these strongholds. I ask for Your mercy and kindness to help me forgive myself, and for the grace to ask forgiveness from others whom I have harmed through my thoughts, words or actions. I now release every evil judgement or unholy perception. I take every vain imagination captive and obedient to Christ. I pray for an infilling of Your power, and authority to edify, encourage, and foster the spirit of Divine love toward all those who enter my life. I thank you for your spirit of peace which unifies us all through the power of Your Holy Spirit. I pray this prayer of intercession for all people of every nation.

Guide my heart, mind and soul to see all of humanity as you do, Jesus. I declare this prayer of healing in my mind and spirit now complete through the power of the Holy Spirit, and the blood covenant of Christ your Son. Amen.

Prayer to Release Strongholds in the Global Church (The Jezebel Spirit)

There are many strong, vibrant, faith-filled, deeply rooted biblical Churches in the United States that are grounded on life-giving principles. My Church is one such body of believers.

Because of its members, and spirit-filled Church leaders, our congregation continues to visibly grow, transform, and reap the fruits of the Holy Spirit. These fruits (when confirmed through the Holy Spirit) are self-evident, scriptural in nature, and show consistent transformation, healing, and Godly service. There are many men, and women leaders in numerous congregations across the United States, both large and small, where God is authentically using them to spread the powerful message of the Gospel of love and healing through compassionate works of service, and the gifts of the Holy Spirit.

Conversely, there are Churches which have unfortunately led members astray. We have seen the effects of sin, or strongholds with leaders in high profile positions, who have taken members down an alternative path, or attracted members through "Christian" showings which falsely represent the spirit, or doctrine of Christ (false behaviors and dogma). As a result, members have experienced confusion or division. Churches have shut down, or members have moved away from God, because of the workings of a powerful spirit called Jezebel.

This spirit, which has been present in the Global Church throughout history, continues to delegitimize the power of Christ's light and love, with those who've been called to lead. It has been responsible for enticing, tempting, and decimating, pastors, priests, ministers, and ministry leaders of God for decades. We see evidence of this spirit in the Old Testament in Kings, through the story of Queen Jezebel, and her seductive, wicked spirit, which not only enticed and murdered the prophets, but spilled the blood of the righteous. This spirit is still present in the modern Church today.

The spirit of Jezebel rears its ugly head through a spirit of seduction, lure, mental or physical violence, enticement, ungodly sexual attraction, and finally, sexual temptation that manifests itself as sexual sin in priests, ministers, pastors, and even lay volunteers as ministry leaders.

You will recognize the spirit is **active** *when there is*;

1. a spirit of evil enticement present, which manifests through the molestation of children;
2. a spirit of adultery present, with illicit affairs going on behind the scenes in the Church;
3. a false or deceptive biblical witness present during Church service, (the spirit of doublemindedness);
4. a spirit of false doctrine which counters biblical truth, that seduces its members to sin, or leads them astray; and
5. a spirit of sexual immortality with priests, ministers, pastors or priests.

We are called to pray and fast for our Church leaders. Our soaking prayers call forth the shield of Christ as a protective covering, petition spiritual strength for them, and implore divine wisdom of the Holy Spirit so they will not fall prey to this seductive spirit.

Pray the Prayer for Release of the Jezebel Spirit with leaders, ministers, pastors, and priests in the Global Church

Lord, we come before you in a spirit of truth, requesting a superior blood covering over the men, and women of God you've called to be visible leaders, and ministers in Your Church. We rise as the people of God, to request a Holy sheltering upon their work, and ministries. We envelope them in Your love, and plead Your protection over each of them now, and forevermore.

We bind all spirits of seduction, enticement, temptation, or sexual immortality from acting in them, through them, or around them under the authority of Your blood, Jesus, and command the presence or influence of the spirit of Jezebel, to immediately cease and desist. Be gone, in the name of Jesus.

We now call forth Michael the Archangel to defend us in this battle. Send your divine light and love throughout our global Church, and its leaders, and ministers, O God, so that they may truly be, *"Your hope and the light of the world."* It is in the name of Jesus we pray, believe and say, Amen.

The Conclusion

As you conclude *The Victory Dance of God*, I believe that God has poured His infinite spirit, love, power, and blessing over you.

You are unique, and wonderfully made. You are truly God's child, His light in a world that is broken. He has called you by name. You are "His." There is no one like you in the entire universe. You are the salt of the earth, and apple of His eye. He has always loved you with an everlasting love from the moment you were conceived in His heart, for Himself, and His ultimate pleasure for all eternity. There is nothing that you can ever do, say, or think, that will ever deter His love for you. It is immeasurable, vast and endless.

There is a grander purpose for your life. My hope and prayer is that you'll discover this purpose and plant your life firmly into the palm of God's hand, and community of the Church where you will grow spiritually; and be loved, affirmed, and cherished. The world is waiting for you to share the riches of your God-given gifts, talents, and the outpouring of your love for Him to others.

I commission you, in the name of Jesus. Go. Find Him. Follow Him.

Lord, break this tender heart, for what breaks yours.

I am often reminded of the beautiful scripture verse that was given to me many years ago, when I was sitting in the seat of my newly visited Church, waiting for service to begin. A young gentleman (whom I did not know) slid over in the seat next to me, and with open bible in hand, pointed to the scripture verse Jeremiah 29: V II. He never said a word to me, and I never saw him again after the service was finished. But the word that was given to me, which became my life verse, was a message of hope that has seemingly lasted a lifetime.

"For I know the plans I have for you," declares the Lord, "plans to prosper you and not to harm you, plans to give you hope and a future."

After Notes

The Proclamation of Promises

1. I John 5 V: 14 - 15

Introduction

1. John 3: V 4
2. Proverbs 27: V 19
3. Luke 6: V 45
4. Ezekiel 36: V 26
5. Job 36: V 11
6. Matthew 19: V 24
7. Jeremiah 29: V 11
8. Mark 9: V 23

Chapter One

1. Matthew 17: V 20
2. John 12 V: 24
3. Ecclesiastes 3 V: 1 - 3
4. 2 Peter 1 V: 3 - 4
5. Matthew 11 V: 19
6. Roman 12 V: 2

7. Philippians 4 V: 13

Chapter Two

1. Corinthians 15: V 55 - 57
2. Philippians 2: V 6 - 8
3. Exodus 3: V 14
4. Matthew 10: V 27
5. ibid. 26: V 52
6. Luke 11: V 11
7. Philippians 4: V 1 - 3
8. Exodus 15: V 26
9. Matthew 6: V 8
10. Deuteronomy 28: V 2
11. Ibid. 29: V 9
12. Psalm 91 V: 1

Chapter Three

Book Mention(s). *To Heaven and Back*, Copyright Mary C. Neal, 2011, 2012., Printed by WaterBrook Press, Colorado Springs, Colorado; United States of America 2012.
Proof of Heaven, Copyright 2012 by Alexander Eben M.D.
1. John 14: V 2
2. Matthew 11: V 28 - 29
3. Jeremiah 30: V 17
4. Romans 12: V 19
5. Proverbs 14: V 15
6. Romans 8: V 6
7. Deuteronomy 31: V 6
8. Exodus 20: V 3
9. Luke 12: V 7
10. John 14: V 6

11. Isaiah 65: V 17
12. Revelation 21: V 1
13. 2 Peter 3: V 13
14. Isaiah 40: V 28 - 31
15. John 10: V 27
16. Proverbs 9: V 10
17. Revelation 21: V 8
18. Matthew 13: V 50
19. Jude 1: V 7
20. Jeremiah 29: V 13
21. Ibid. 1: V 4

Chapter Four

1. Luke 18: V 35 - 42
2. John 14: V 12
3. Ibid. 4: V 37
4. 1 Corinthians 13: V 12
5. Acts 3: V 17 - 18
6. Psalm 98: V 1
7. Matthew 19: V 26
8. Daniel 3: V 16 - 18
9. Jeremiah 29: V 11
10. 2 Corinthians 10: V 7 - 8
11. Ephesians 1: V 7 - 8
12. 2 Corinthians 12: V 9
13. 1 Peter 5: V 10
14. Mark 9: V 23

Chapter Five

1. Psalm 27: V 14
2. Psalm 91: V 14 - 16

3. Hebrew 10: V 35 - 36
4. Jeremiah 29: V 11 referenced, paraphrased
5. 2 Thessalonians 2: V 15 - 17
6. Psalm 27: V 14
7. Philippians 4: V 6 - 7
8. Romans 8: V 26 - 27
9. James 5: V 16
10. Psalm 9: V 5
11. Isaiah 30: V 21

Chapter Six

1. Ephesians 6: V 14 - 17
2. Ibid. 1: V 19 - 22
3. Mark 1: V 13
4. Revelation 12: V 10
5. 1 Peter 5: V 8
6. Revelation 2: V 10
7. 1 Peter 5: V 8
8. Matthew 4: V 3
9. Ephesians 6: V 16
10. John 10: V 10
11. Revelation 9: V1
12. Colossians 1: V 9
13. 2 Thessalonians 2: V 3 - 4
14. Isaiah 14: V 12 - 14
15. John 8: V 44
16. 2 Corinthians 10: V 4
17. James 1: V 8
18. Psalm 119: V 113 - 115
19. Romans 5: V 2
20. Ephesians 6: V 12
21. Ibid. 2: V 2
22. Genesis 3: V 1 - 4

23. Acts 9: V 1 - 2
24. Ibid. V 3 - 5
25. Ephesians 6: V 10 - 18
26. Ibid. 6: V 13 - 17
27. John 10: V 10
28. 2 Corinthians 10: V 4

Chapter Seven

1. Hebrew 4: V 12
2. John 1: V 1
3. 2 Corinthians 5: V 8
4. Isaiah 43: V 1
5. Joel 2: V 28
6. Jeremiah 33: V 3
7. Hebrews 13: V 15
8. Affirmations based on Psalms 1 through 21

Chapter Eight

1. Ezekiel 7: V 23

Conclusion

1. Jeremiah 29: V 11

More About the Author

Mary Frances McMahon is a founder and president of NFTN, (Nurses for the Nations), a Christian, 501 (c) (3) nonprofit, global ministry comprised of diverse healthcare, and lay professionals who serve global communities cut off from compassionate medical and nursing care, and the message of the Gospel. Nurses for the Nations has served over 12,000 men, women, and children internationally since its launch in 2008 through compassionate care and performed local outreach to men, women and children in the Savannah community.

In 2017, NFTN officially launched its local outreach ministry called Neighborhood H.O.P.E. (Health, Outreach, Professions, and Evangelism). The community branch offers health and wellness activities which support, engage, and educate the public on disease, and other issues.

Mary is a devoted wife to her husband Bob, 'mom,' grandma, nurse, teacher, trainer, Christian speaker, and ministry leader.

In-between family life and work duties, Mary enjoys think-tank nature walks, watching warm sunsets, and pursuing early morning writing projects when ideas are fresh, and blessings flow freely from the pen. She resides in Georgia with her husband Bob. You may contact the author by e-mail correspondence through the ministry of NFTN at info@nursesforthenations.org

About the Ministry

NFTN is financially supported by the public as well its affiliation with Compassion Christian Church (CCC) in Savannah, Georgia. The authors home Church is comprised of seven active worship campuses, and a membership following that is over 11,000 strong.

Ten-percent of proceeds from the Book, *The Victory Dance of God, His Promise of Healing is Yours,* will be personally donated by the author to the Compassion Christian Church, Global Outreach Department in Savannah, Georgia, to be used for the continued work of discipleship, and spreading of the Gospel throughout the world. An additional ten-percent of the proceeds will be donated by the author to NFTN (Nurses for the Nations) to continue the work of ministry through medical and nursing care, education and training for men, women, and children cut off from receiving compassionate help; all while promoting the tangible message of the Gospel of healing to those who need it.

Learn more about the ministry of NFTN and its local and international activities by going to www.nursesforthenations.org. Read about the author and leadership board members at http://www.nursesforthenations.org/about-us/our-board/

Plug into our compassionate work at NFTN, by joining a local group as a volunteer through Neighborhood H.O.P.E. (Health, Outreach, Professions, Evangelism). Contact us at info@nursesforthenations.org

Finally, sow a compassionate seed! By purchasing this book, you are promoting the work of the Gospel, and allowing professional, and lay service team members to bring medical, and nursing care to remote areas of the world. Be a part of our continuum of hope and healing to the poor communities we serve by planting a financial seed at www.nursesforthenations.org Click on DONATE.

Why not purchase this book as a gift for a family member or friend? God will bless you ten-fold when you give for the cause!

NFTN is an all-volunteer nonprofit ministry. Ninety-eight percent of all NFTN's donations go directly to the front lines to assist others locally, and internationally. You may visit the website for NFTN's financials'.

Printed in the United States
By Bookmasters